# JEWELS OF LIGHT

by Emory John Michael

*Dear Jan,*
*Peace and joy*
*on the journey!*
*Emory John Michael*

Mountain Rose Publishing
PO Box 2738
Prescott, AZ 86302

JEWELS OF LIGHT
by Emory J. Michael

Mountain Rose Publishing
Prescott, Arizona

First Edition Copyright © Emory J. Michael 1997

Mountain Rose Publishing
P.O. Box 2738
Prescott, AZ  86302
520-445-5056

ISBN 0-9642147-1-7  First Edition - 1997

Printed in the United States of America at
Graphic Impressions, Prescott, Arizona.

Typesetting and layout by
Aardvark Graphic & Type, Prescott, Arizona.

Cover design by Emory J. Michael and Mia Michael.

Address all correspondence to Emory J. Michael,
care of Mountain Rose Publishing.

10, 9, 8, 7, 6, 5, 4, 3, 2, 1

## PRELUDE

There was once a tiny mountain surrounded by many high mountains. The small mountain looked with envy at the tall, majestic peaks that towered above it. In the winter the large peaks were covered with snow and people came from far and wide to ski on the beautiful slopes. In the summer, adventurers enjoyed climbing the impressive rocks, campers explored the high trails and valleys, and children played on the meadows.

The tiny mountain felt ignored, unappreciated, and unloved. Then one day some people came and drilled several deep holes into her interior. They were excited by what they found. Soon many visitors came to see the small peak. It was declared a national treasure, for it was discovered that the tiny mountain was filled with gold, diamonds, and all manner of precious gemstones and jewels. The tiny mountain beamed with happiness and pride to know that deep within she had such a vast store of hidden treasures.

Each of us is like the little mountain in this simple tale. Within us is a priceless treasure—the jewels of our soul and spirit. This book is a tool to help you uncover the splendor that lies within you.

# CONTENTS

## Acknowledgments

Special thanks to Katie and Abe for their boundless generosity. To my wife, Mia, who is a beacon of light and a constant inspiration, and to my daughter, Sera Maria—one of my wisest teachers and a source of wonder and delight—I express eternal gratitude. Thank you for believing.

# INTRODUCTION

One day a man of about sixty came into my wife's and my bookshop. I greeted him and told him that if he needed any help would he please let me know. He paused a moment, then with a half smile and a gleam in his eye replied, "All I need is a sack of jewels and a second chance."

I loved his response, and have always felt that those few words speak volumes about the human condition. Virtually all of us would like to have a "sack of jewels" with which to "finance" our lives, whether we conceive of those "jewels" as being in the form of money, health, position, beauty, education, or talent. And virtually everyone would like to be able to re-live certain experiences or periods of life, for nearly all of us carry regrets or feel that we've "botched" at least a few things along our journey.

The fact is that the greatest "jewels" and the most valuable treasures are not of a material nature. They are the insights we gain into the laws and principles that govern life, the "pearls beyond price" of higher understanding. These truths are the bedrock of creation. They are the foundation of happiness and successful living. By living in accordance with these truths, miracles are possible.

When people transform themselves by applying these insights they become truly rich. In so doing they remold their character and unlock an inner storehouse of spiritual treasures. If all things of a material nature were then taken from such individuals—leaving them destitute, penniless, and alone—by applying these ideas they could within a short period of time regain what they had lost. The real jewels of life consist of these inner riches of the spirit, "treasures in heaven" that are available to all human beings.

And though it's true we can't go back into the past and re-live our life again—except in our imagination—we can begin anew each moment to fashion the kind of future we want. It's never too late to begin applying the deeper truths of life. In Tennyson's great poem, *Ulysses*, the old hero speaks words of wisdom for us all. Ulysses stands at the end of his days, still seeking adventure and truth, and passionately tells his followers that "it's not too late to seek a newer world."

It seems that many people today stumble through their experiences, unaware of the deeper laws and principles upon which life is organized. As the years pass, the regret and the bitterness accumulate. Perhaps this is the dark side of our vaunted "age of information." There is such an overwhelming outpouring of disconnected "facts" that it is easy for these ageless truths to get lost in our culture's information labyrinth. Sadly, a multitude of people never seem to "get the message."

Many years ago, when I was struggling to figure out what life was all about, I had the good fortune to meet an unusual man whom I would describe as a "practical mystic"—someone intimately acquainted with his true self, yet firmly grounded in earth realities. He was a teacher of ancient history and his specialty was Egyptology. He had also been a life-long student of comparative religion. Though seeming fairly "ordinary" to casual observation, in his conversation he displayed a ripened wisdom which was the fruit of life-long efforts to grasp the deeper truths of existence—

truths which are the foundation stone of wisdom underlying human culture. It was the early seventies, a time of great social agitation, and this man was particularly sensitive to the issues of the period. Yet he seemed to have achieved a degree of serenity and inner contentment that made a deep impression on me.

One day I had a lengthy conversation with him. We talked about the problems in the world—and about the mysterious "hidden splendor" within all people. He said most people lived life as if they were in a dark cave underground and had forgotten about the sunny atmosphere outside the cave—a luminous world which is our true home. He challenged me to come out of the darkness and discover the bright realm outside the cave of ignorance, a realm he appeared to know intimately. He claimed that there was a body of essential truths that formed the core of all religions, both ancient and modern, and that the science of the future would be based on these insights—the essence of which has been called *the perennial philosophy*. He called these ideas the secrets of existence. When we begin to master these truths, he explained, we step outside the dark cave into the brightness of the world that we have forgotten, the land of light from which we have come. I found our conversation stimulating and enlightening.

The next day I was startled when he gave me a lengthy handwritten essay on the very subjects we had discussed the previous evening. It was entitled, "Jewels of Enlightened Living." He had apparently spent much of the night writing the material for my benefit. I was deeply touched by his gesture. I poured over his writings, finding them illuminating. It was a sketch of ancient wisdom embellished with his personal realizations. He had captured in those few pages the essence of what for me was—and remains to this day—a philosophy of happiness. I have never seen him since, but have often thought of our conversation, and the "jewels" that he gave me.

In the spirit of the teacher who wrote those inspired pages years ago for my benefit and instruction, I offer this book in the hope that it will be found useful as a condensation of this ageless and eternally living philosophy. My wish is that it will contribute toward a broader understanding of these principles. This work is based on my efforts of the past 27 years to build my life on a knowledge of these laws—truths which I believe are the heart of the wisdom of antiquity as well as the foundation of the new consciousness. Each of these laws is like a letter in nature's alphabet which helps us read the living book of truth that lies before us each day. The chapters that follow contain descriptions of twelve of the most significant truths—one might call them "perspectives"—of enlightened living, magical "jewels" that lead to a more luminous life.

Throughout human history, jewels and gemstones have been among the most prized of all precious things. Symbolically, they have always represented wisdom, love and truth—the everlasting elements of higher knowledge. The discovery of these "jewels of the spirit" helps us to live prosperously and successfully—and to make the world a better place. This is done when we grasp the laws of life with our minds, express them in our relationships, and *live* them in our actions.

Those who can activate the power represented by each "jewel" begin to experience a transformation. It is as if they are each handed the keys to a kingdom all their own—a realm of limitless possibilities where they are destined to reign masterfully. They become creative and successful in their lives. Most important of all, they are led to the discovery of life's greatest treasure, the immortal jewel of the indwelling spirit.

May the ideas in this book help you discover the keys to your kingdom.

Emory John Michael — January, 1997

Dedicated to the Messengers of Light of all times and places.

## A Personal Note

In October of 1993, I self-published an autobiographical work of fiction entitled, QUEEN OF THE SUN. When the book arrived from the printer, I tossed some boxes into my van and drove to bookstores in Arizona and New Mexico, selling my book to whoever would take it. In December and January several book distributors began to supply QUEEN and sales picked up in the independent bookstore market. Just a few weeks later, in mid February, I received a call from a prominent literary agent in California. She told me that she had seen my book and felt it had the potential to be a national bestseller. In short, she wanted to be my agent. I was thrilled, for I knew that she represented several very successful writers, some of whose books were on the New York Times bestseller list.

Just days later she had to take an unexpected, month-long leave of absence from her work and suggested I not wait for her, because, in her words, "things happen very quickly in this business." I hired another California agent she recommended and a week later we received a substantial offer from a large publishing house. It was a dream come true.

As part of the preparation for a 12-city publicity tour to promote QUEEN, my publisher flew me to Los Angeles to receive "media training." I was told that as part of the promotional efforts for QUEEN OF THE SUN, I would need to "tell my personal story." I found that to be a challenge, for I was reticent about talking about myself in front of groups. I realized that growing up in my family, I had not been encouraged to "promote" myself. Not that I was actively discouraged, but the subtle message was that it wasn't dignified to make yourself the subject of the conversation.

But the fact is that all of us are interested in each other's story. Each person's biography communicates something of the universally human. We learn from each other and from our trials, failures, and successes. Each of us is on the same journey in life, the journey to our deeper selves, which, in the language of mysticism, is also the journey to God.

I don't think my childhood was particularly unusual, but I had one memorable event which stands out in my mind because of its vivid and extraordinary nature. When I was five years old, I lived with my parents and four brothers in a small town in Connecticut. One sunny spring morning I was walking across the parking lot to my red-brick apartment when I became aware of a "presence" behind me. I turned around, but there was no one there. My sense of the "presence" remained, however, and became still stronger. Although there was nothing perceivable to my physical senses, I *knew* there was someone standing beside me. I felt an overwhelming sense of security and well-being. Whoever this "presence" was, she or he was unimaginably loving and protective. The "presence" then "spoke" to me, not in physically audible words, but in a clear and powerful thought that filled my entire being with an energy and an awareness I had never known. The presence said simply, "You are on earth to learn to love."

I stood still for a moment, serenely happy, conscious that the experience was an "unusual" one. Although at that age I did not have a conceptual framework in which to place the event, I knew that something important had just transpired. I ran across the parking lot to my apartment, filled with an overwhelming happiness. Even at the age of five, I somehow sensed that I had been given the deeper purpose of my life. I never mentioned the experience to anyone, but filed it away, referring back to it in times of disappointment, loneliness, and fear.

In my late teens, when I began to read spiritual and metaphysical literature, I came across the concept of a "guardian angel." I am now quite certain that my guardian angel had drawn close to me, made me aware of its loving presence, and "communicated" that beautiful thought to my childhood mind. I believe that one reason I was given the experience was so that I would develop the conviction that the physical world was not the only reality. It was not until I was nineteen years old that I would again have a similar experience.

It was 1970, and American society was more deeply divided than at any time since the Civil War. The Viet Nam conflict was raging and claiming 250 American lives per week. The so-called "counter-culture" of the disenchanted "sixties generation" had begun to experiment in eastern mysticism and "alternative lifestyles." The use of psychedelic drugs, marijuana, and a whole list of other "mind-altering" substances was epidemic, and had spilled over into the mainstream. I had smoked grass a couple of times during my freshman year at college. During the summer of 1969 I got high more frequently and took LSD for the first time at the legendary Woodstock music festival in New York state. During my sophomore year at college, it seemed wherever I went someone was passing a pipe or rolling a "joint." I smoked grass or hashish nearly everyday. At the same time, I started to become interested in mystical spirituality. My psychology professor, a wonderfully intuitive educator named Richard Perls, played to us the taped lectures of Baba Ram Dass—formerly Richard Alpert of Harvard—who had just returned from his sojourn with a spiritual master in India. I knew there was another world, the world of the spirit, that was calling to me. Intuitions from my deeper self told me that I had to leave drugs behind if I wanted to truly live a more spiritual life, but I had become addicted to the experience.

In May of 1970, four students were killed by National Guardsmen who opened fire at an anti-war protest at Kent State University in Ohio. My friends and I were stunned. A huge protest was planned for the University of Maryland in College Park the next weekend. My life was about to change dramatically.

One morning that week I was in the Montgomery College cafeteria in Tacoma Park, Maryland. As I walked slowly across the floor to leave the building, I was overcome with an aware-ness of the same benign "presence" that had visited me when I was a five-year-old boy near my home in Connecticut. The "presence" radiated extraordinary power, and again I "heard" a thought ring through my whole being. But this time the message was not so pleasant. "Find your direction or you will not remain on earth much longer." I knew that the message had to do with discovering my task on earth, and felt it was a specific warning to stop using drugs. Although moved by the feeling of compas-sion that I sensed from the visiting "presence," who I believed was my angel, I was shaken and disturbed by the content of the angel's message.

That same week I had an unusually vivid and remarkable

dream. In the dream I was riding an old bicycle—the first I had ever owned as a child—past my old high school. I was on the wrong side of the road and a huge truck was coming straight at me. I was unable to get out of the way of the truck and we collided violently. At the moment of "impact," I awoke from the dream, sweating and shaken. Although I had never read books on dream analysis, I knew intuitively what this dream was telling me: change my life direction or lose my life.

That Saturday afternoon I gathered with friends at College Park for the antiwar protest. In the wake of the Kent State shootings, the mood of the crowd was restless and many people were angry. The National Guard was there in force and there was danger of another tragic incident. Thousands of people of all ages and walks of life blocked off Route One. I sat in the road in a semicircle with some friends. A young man was playing guitar and someone passed a marijuana "joint' around the circle. With my recent vivid dream and the experience of the "angel presence" still strongly in my mind, a powerful intuition told me not to partake. But I suppressed the "still small voice," telling myself that one more time wouldn't matter. Moments after inhaling, I began to experience sensations I had never had from marijuana or any other drug. They were somewhat pleasurable, but accompanied by a touch of nausea. When the joint came around a second time I took another long inhale. Moments later, I knew I had made a mistake.

The feelings of nausea increased and became unbearable. I felt a terrible pressure in my head and a feeling of sickness throughout my body. The sound of the guitar was like an actual physical force grating against every cell. I had never felt so terrible in my life. Shortly thereafter I passed out of external con-

sciousness and entered an "internal" world of horrific darkness. I
was certain that I had died and apparently had entered into the
very pit of hell. I can only describe the experience as that of being
ground up and pulverized into tiny fragments.

Slowly I left this dark region and seemed to rise toward a
place of greater light. The terrible feelings left me, although I still
felt that I was in a kind of limbo region, suspended between a
world of luminosity above me and the terrible region of darkness
out of which I had just ascended. Slowly I felt myself drawn
upward into the region of light, and as I entered this atmosphere
my feeling of joy and rapture increased. Moments later I was
engulfed in a sea of blissful happiness such as I had never experienced before.

Slowly I lost consciousness in this luminous world. In fact, I
lost consciousness completely. When I finally awoke, perhaps
twenty minutes after the experience began, my friends were
overjoyed, for they were afraid that I would never regain consciousness from my bizarre reaction to the joint, which had
apparently been laced with some chemical. No one else had been
adversely affected, but I am convinced that if I had taken another "hit" I would have died.

Since that time I have read dozens of books which describe
the "classic" near-death experience. Although I wish I could say I
encountered a "being of light" and had seen my entire life pass
before my eyes, I must admit that my experience was different.
But I did become aware—when I entered the region of light and
happiness—of the "presence" of the angel who had come to me
when I was five years old and had warned me just days earlier
that I needed to "change my path."

I radically altered my life in the months following my close brush with death. I became a vegetarian and began to read every book on spiritual matters I could find. I started to pray and meditate earnestly every day. Shortly before my twentieth birthday, I read the *Bhagavhad Gita*, the great spiritual epic of India, four times in a month. It felt as if the scales were dropping from my eyes and I was discovering the spiritual world of light for which I hungered. I also read several classics of Christian mysticism including *Dark Night of the Soul*, by the Spanish mystic, St. John of the Cross; *Imitation of Christ*, by Thomas à Kempis, and the anonymously written, *Cloud of Unknowing*. I was profoundly impressed with these works. Although I didn't stop using marijuana overnight, within five months I no longer felt the desire to smoke. The practices of prayer and meditation had enabled me to stop.

In the spring of 1971, I felt I needed to have the kind of mystical revelation I had been reading about. I decided to go into the forest by myself in hopes of having a transforming inner experience. As part of my preparation I gave away virtually all of my possessions other than some books, clothes, and a minimum of equipment that I would need for camping. I then headed into the woods of Virginia and camped for several days, fasting, praying, and reading illuminating books, spending most of my time with *The Cloud Of Unknowing*, and a tiny book containing all the words of Christ from the New Testament.

On the second day I heard a loud crashing in the woods. I had heard of the Native American practice of the vision quest, and was aware that during the traditional four day vigil one was often visited by an animal, which became of great importance to one's life. It occurred to me that perhaps I was about to receive a visit from my "power animal." As a result, I was rather disappointed to discover that the animal responsible for the racket in the woods was a large Virginia wild turkey.

But the next day I had another visitor, this time a large tawny animal that I glimpsed through the screen of underbrush in front of me. The animal made a strange grumbling sound in its throat and slammed its front paw or hoof hard into the ground. It seemed a bellicose gesture, a sign that this creature didn't want me there. The frightening image of a mountain lion flashed in my mind, but I had never heard of one coming so far east.

Moments later a large stag deer with threatening antlers crashed through the underbrush just a few feet away from where I sat cross-legged on a blanket, then bounded into the woods. Although at first I didn't attach much importance to the animal visitations, their significance increased as time wore on. It was several years later that I discovered that in the Native American tradition, the turkey represents the "give-away." It symbolizes generosity and the ability to give of oneself, knowing that the universal supply will always bring you what you need. This seemed remarkable in light of the fact I had given nearly away all my material possessions just days before leaving on my "vision quest" into the Virginia forest. I also discovered that a male deer was a symbol of strength and independence, both qualities I needed at the time. And I was to later discover that antlers and horns, whether they appear in symbolism or in art, represent the development of higher faculties of perception, the clairvoyant gifts of the spirit that exist potentially in all human beings. In retrospect I can see that these two animals in their symbolic natures have been significant for my entire life. For "giving" has always seemed to me the essence of the fundamental moral law on which this universe rests. And my entire adult life has been an effort to

awaken awareness of the deeper self, which leads to the unfolding of clairvoyant and intuitive gifts of spirit.

That summer I hitch-hiked across country from Maryland to
California and back, having marvelous experiences and meeting
extraordinary people along the way. Immediately upon my return
to the east coast, I made preparations to leave for Peru. I was
intent on finding an ancient spiritual retreat which I had read of
in the unusual book, now out-of-print, entitled *Secret of the
Andes*. I went with two friends, Ed and Charles.

That experience in the Andes deserves a book of its own, and
in many ways became the inspiration for QUEEN OF THE SUN.
The effort of hiking in the high Andes for weeks at a time was
both transformative and exhausting. Ed returned to the states
first and my parents sent me a plane ticket about a month later.
Charles intended to remain in Peru and continue his search for
the valley. In the charming town of Juliaca, over fourteen thousand feet above sea level, I gave Charles the last of my money and
hugged him goodbye.

During the next several months, I received several letters
from Charles in which he described his experiences and the people he encountered. In particular, he mentioned a young woman
named Sal, who was also in search of the valley and with whom
he had met up. Then the letters from Charles abruptly stopped.
I had a vague intuition that something unpleasant had happened
to him.

That summer, while I was working in a natural foods restaurant in Washington, DC, called *YES!*, I gradually became aware of
a peculiar phenomenon. On numerous occasions my attention
was drawn to a particular, dark-haired young woman. I would see
her walking along the streets, browsing in shops, even passing in

cars. The experience was uncanny, for it was unusual to keep
noticing the same person in a variety of places and situations in a
sprawling city of more than a million people. It was as if I was
being prepared to meet her. One day she and I actually met for
the first time in *Yes!* bookstore. We were astonished to learn that
we had both recently returned from Peru. The shocker came
when we finally exchanged names. She was Sal!

In a few breathless minutes I caught up on the events in
Charles' life since I had left him in the high Andes several months
earlier. To my dismay, I learned why the letters from Charles had
abruptly ended. He had gone down a llama trail against the plead-
ing of the Quechua Indian guide and the others in the group,
which included Sal. Charles was never seen again.

Both Sal and I felt intuitively that Charles was no longer alive
on earth. But we needed confirmation. We had heard of a rep-
utable medium who lived in Washington not far from the Capitol
building. We made an appointment to see her.

A stocky blondhaired woman with a German accent met us
warmly at the door and ushered us into her apartment. Her name
was Irmgard. She knew nothing about the reason of our visit and
we had told her nothing about ourselves or about Charles. We sat
at a small table and Irmgard said the Lord's Prayer, then entered
a meditative state, though remaining fully conscious. Within
moments of my handing her Charles' letter she began to tell us in
great detail exactly what had happened to him. She said Charles
had stumbled on the trail and fallen to his death on the mountain
side. He had died instantly and was "in the light." He was happy
except for the fact that his parents missed him. He regretted
leaving earth without having healed his relationship with his
father. Now his father was about to hire private detectives and

organize a search for his missing son. Through the mediumship of Irmgard, Charles asked Sal and I to visit his parents and "tell them what had happened." Sal and I were absolutely convinced of the authenticity of the message. We were certain that we had spoken with Charles.

Visiting Charles' parents, whom we had never met before, was one of the most difficult things I have ever done. They were cordial and happy to meet two young people who had recently spent time with their missing son. But it was obviously difficult for them to have lost communication with him. They were practicing Roman Catholics and we wished to respect their beliefs. We did not feel it appropriate to simply blurt out that "Charles had spoken to us" through a medium. In 1972, young people who professed to communicate with "spirits on the other side" were still a rather suspect group. But we also felt compelled to tell them our intuitions, now confirmed in the session with Irmgard, and to honor Charles' request to us through the medium. With as much delicacy as we could muster, we shared our conviction that Charles had "died," but was "alive and well" in the spiritual dimensions.

Years later, when I was living outside Rome, Italy, I was alone one autumn night in my apartment. As I sat at my desk, preparing lessons for the fifth grade class I was teaching in a small, English-speaking international school, I had a profound sense of Charles' presence in the room. I felt that he wanted me to communicate with his parents. That night I wrote a long letter to his mother, stating again my conviction that Charles had left this earth life while hiking in the Andes. I also expressed my strong beliefs that life on earth was a reflection of the greater existence of which we are a part, and that in our soul and spiritual nature we can never die. Some months later I received a letter from her in which she thanked me and stated her intuition that Charles had indeed passed from this earth. I also realized in retrospect that the night that I had been so filled with a sense of Charles' presence in my apartment was November first, All Soul's Night, the time when traditionally the spirits of the departed are allowed to come near their loved ones on earth.

We live our earthly lives on the borderland of luminous eternity, yet most people pass their existence in "outer darkness," ignorant of the great mystery. Since my teen years I have always felt close to the "higher" realms from which we have come. For me the real and true world has always been the "hidden side" and my challenge has been to "get a grip" on material existence. I have learned that we are not here to escape our tasks and responsibilities by ignoring earthly life, something not easy for a person with strong mystical inclinations. Rather, our task is to transform the earth by applying the eternal laws of life in all our efforts, even the seemingly most mundane. We are here to master earthly life by infusing the spirit into our work. To do this we need to employ what we gain from prayer and meditation, learning to work with physical vitality, strength, and energy. It is not easy to find the balance between material pursuits and spiritual fulfillment, but it is possible when we discover and apply life's dynamic underlying principles. When we live these truths, we awaken our "hidden self," the sleeping giant of our immortal spirit.

In fact, our deeper self is already awake. The path of inner unfolding consists largely in shrugging off the cultural trance in which our personalities slumber. We dissolve the mist of illusion—the "cloud of unknowing"—that lies between our conscious mind and our "divine spark" when we comprehend and live the eternal laws. I hope my efforts to delineate these laws as I have come to know them will help the reader find their own "heaven on earth."

## Prayer to a Guardian Angel

*Be thou a shining star above me.*
*Be thou a shepherd to protect me.*
*Be thou a guiding light to lead me.*
*Be thou a rose of love within me.*
*Be thou a beauty shining through me.*
*Be above, below, beside, before, behind me.*
*Be all around about me.*

— Traditional Celtic

# CHAPTER ONE
## The First Jewel — The Magic of the Seed

*"A man must put grain in the ground before he can harvest."*
— Gypsy proverb

*"As is the gardener, so is the garden."* — Jewish proverb

*"I am going to broadcast the seed and let the wind carry it where it will."* — Teilhard de Chardin

*"Give and it shall be given unto you."* — Jesus

An old man at the end of his years sits and rummages through the musty mementos and artifacts of his life. Gazing at old letters, papers, and photographs, he becomes increasingly wistful. Tears fill his eyes. He feels that despite the richness of his experience, some secret of happiness has eluded him. He cannot shake the heavy sense of emptiness—almost a feeling of despair—of having missed out on some essence or insight into life that could have brought fulfillment.

An image comes to the old man of one of his favorite boyhood stories, the tale of Aladdin and his magical lamp. "If only such a lamp had actually existed!" he laments. Perhaps then, if he had found such a lamp, his fondest dreams would have been achieved.

Sadly, the old man had never realized that such a lamp was always within his reach.

Most men and women go through life as if asleep or in a dream, never quite reaching the secret goals of their hearts, or even of clearly defining what these goals are. Yet like the old man in the above example, each of us has within our grasp an Aladdin's lamp of limitless power. Those who discover this power become masters of their world and reign supreme over the conditions of life. What is this mythic force, this secret amulet, with which we may fashion the world of our dreams?

Modern physics claims that our galaxy came into being through the activity of "super novas," the mysterious birth of stars. The physical matter of which our bodies are made—the atomic elements of which our organisms are composed—originated in these fiery nuclear reactions within stars. In our physical constitution we are literally "star dust." Paralleling this material view of modern science, the wisdom of the ancient teachings of both western and eastern spirituality—the essence of the culture of antiquity—states that each individual is endowed with a "divine spark," a spiritual flame fashioned from the primordial Light by those Creative Spirits who brought the universe, in both its spiritual and material aspects, into being.

The lamp of the old man's dreams represents this extraordinary power hidden away within our minds and souls. The genie of the lamp signifies the spiritual spark which is the core essence of all individuals. Socrates, the wise Athenian philosopher who gave so much to civilization, called this deeper self his "daimon." Today it is often called the Higher Self or "indwelling presence."

Regardless of the terms we use, this mysterious core identity is the source of life, energy, love, and power which lights all human beings that come into the world. The way to invoke the genie of the lamp lies in the way we live our life. We rub the lamp by an understanding of the laws that govern existence, and by applying these truths in daily living. Each person holds the key of destiny in his or her hands.

Despite the many conflicting views regarding an ultimate Higher Power in the cosmos, it is obvious that a remarkable intelligence has organized the world. The universe in which we live is fashioned out of a profound genius and a measureless love. There is an underlying wisdom in life, a system of celestial laws or heavenly principles not created by humans, but which all of us may discover if we so desire. These are the laws of our own being and are the building blocks of the manifested universe.

No doubt, Cosmic Intelligence would like us to succeed—to be healthy, happy and fulfilled. But the universe will not simply give us what we want without effort on our part. We must learn to work with the laws upon which life is organized. We are free to create the kind of life we desire, but there is a price to pay. The universe demands that we live in harmony with the underlying principles which govern life. A magical awakening takes place in all those who aspire to comprehend these eternal laws. By living in accord with these truths, one awakens life-bestowing forces in both heart and mind. New perceptions arise, and these find expression in a more expanded and more subtle intelligence. A universal harmony may be perceived, perhaps for the first time.

The fundamental law of life is the law of the seed. Gardeners were the first philosophers. Gardeners know that they can only harvest what they have first planted. They know that it is no use bemoaning fate if there are no carrots to harvest at the end of the growing season. If they want carrots, they must plant them.

So it is in life. Each life is like a garden, and we can only reap what we have sown. Our experiences are a fertile field in which we are always planting seeds. The seeds we sow each day in the soil of our life are our thoughts, words, feelings, and deeds. Just as gardeners can only harvest what they have first planted, so can we only take out of our lives what we have put into them. The kinds of seeds you sow will determine the harvest.

This law of the seed is the essential law, the root principle of life. In a sense, knowledge of this dynamic truth is the "philosopher's stone," the magic talisman that can bring us what we want. It may not turn lead to gold, but it can transform one's life from dullness and frustration to expectation and success. By comprehending and applying this principle, you can establish your life on a new footing and free yourself from the negativity of the age that is dying.

The law of the seed is the law of causation. In physics this law is expressed as Newton's third law of motion: for every action there is an equal reaction—equal in force and opposite in direction. This law is at work everywhere in the realms of human experience and relationship. Those fortunate individuals who truly grasp and embrace this law gain the power to completely transform their health, their finances, their relationships, their spiritual understanding, and their career.

Action does not mean physical action only. Whenever we think, feel, or speak we set in motion the delicate mechanism of reciprocity. Thus we are always planting seeds. If not with our hands, then with our minds and our hearts, our words and our decisions. In the short term, our behavior impacts those around

us. In the end, our deeds come home to roost. We receive into
our lives the very currents we ourselves have released into the
ocean of existence.

For every action there is a consequence, every decision we
make leads to a whole string of ensuing events. Every deed plants
a seed, every consequence of action is the fruit of the seed.
Sowing and reaping are linked together as two aspects of the
same operation. Everything we receive in life is directly connected to the forces we have set in motion by what we do. All reaping is a direct consequence of the actions of head, heart, and
hands. All that we obtain in life is rooted in our behavior.

Maturity in life begins when we start to take responsibility for
the circumstances in which we find ourselves. This is no easy
task, for as one wit put it, "To err is human, to blame others is
even more human." We step on to the path of wisdom when we
take charge of our own affairs. Truly, there is no one to blame. No
matter how rough or how peaceful the seas, each one of us guides
the rudder that steers the ship of our life.

Virtually everyone falls short of their ideal of what—or *who*—
they'd like to be. Our culture puts such an emphasis on external
beauty that nearly everybody feels a bit *less than* on occasion.
Most women aren't naturally drop-dead gorgeous. And most men
resemble Moe, Larry or Curly more closely than a heart throb
from the soaps. But we must realize that the source of life experience is within us. Not only does intelligence spring from within, so also do authentic beauty, spiritual understanding, and—ultimately—happiness. It has been said that happiness is an inside
job. The same may be said for beauty, intelligence, and success—
however we may define them. They are all "inside jobs." When
we change our thoughts, feelings, and attitudes, we change our

life experience from within. This inner change begins when we grasp and apply the law of the seed.

Regardless of where we find ourselves in the stream of life, we can begin now to remold ourselves in the image of our idealism by applying this dynamic principle—the law of the seed. Seeming miracles of inner and outer transformation can occur if we are willing to work with this and the other ideas described in this book.

An acquaintance of mine turned his fortunes around by applying this principle of the seed. Tom's life had spun out of control as a result of his drinking and his habitual negativity. He lost his job and his wife left him. Nobody liked to be around him for he never had anything good to say about anything. He was in a downward spiral with no end in sight when he wandered into the public library one day to get out of the rain. He fell to reading the classic book by James Allen, *As a Man Thinketh*, which a friend had once recommended to him. He spent the entire day absorbing the book, then bought a copy of his own the next day. He was so influenced by the book's message that he wanted everyone to know about the philosophy it contained. He arranged with a bookstore to buy fifty copies at a discount, and these he began to give away to people on the street, in stores, to whomever he got in a conversation with. Through AA he got sober, and as a result of his remarkable reversal in attitude he completely reversed his fortunes. He volunteered his time helping out in a metaphysical bookstore, and soon got a job there. When I knew him it was difficult to imagine the straits in which he had once been trapped, for he was universally admired and respected for his sunny disposition and his generosity.

The law of the seed is life's central and most dynamic principle. Without a comprehension of this law, life is a bewildering maze of haphazard and unrelated accidents—all "sound and fury, signifying nothing." A knowledge of this truth is the golden thread that can lead one out of the labyrinth of ignorance, into the clear light of understanding. It has been called the law of the echo, for life echoes back to us all that we send forth into the world. Like a boomerang, the consequences of our actions do indeed return to us, either to help or to haunt. Our thoughts and deeds in the present have value and importance for all time to come.

Modern physics is beginning to corroborate what sages taught in the temples of ancient times, that our universe is a universe of light. There exists everywhere a delicate recording mechanism, a subtle luminous membrane that interpenetrates all things physical. Upon this sensitive layer, or energy field—called the *quintessence* by ancient Greek philosophers, *akasha* in Sanskrit, and "the Book of God's Remembrance" in the Bible—all thoughts, feelings, words and actions are imprinted, just as you leave footprints when you walk on the beach. The universe records all things and keeps a just account of all our sowing and reaping throughout time. We might think of this subtle recording mechanism as a kind of universal bookkeeping system which records infallibly every transaction of our lives. The condition of our account will determine our circumstances, including the level of our prosperity.

In the east, the balance of our account is called *karma*. In the west we call it *fate*, or *fortune*. The wheel of fortune spins in everyone's life. If you don't like where the wheel has stopped, you can give it another turn. It is not a frozen wheel. No one ever condemns another person to an unhappy life. Each of us pronounce our own sentence.

If you feel that life has dealt you a bad hand, deal yourself a new hand. Start to create better conditions now by setting in motion currents of constructive force through positive, helpful thoughts and acts. Plant beneficial seeds with all that you do.

When my wife, Mia, and I started our first bookstore in California it was a dream come true. But the first few months were a real struggle. We had very little capital and virtually nothing to spend on advertising. Business was slow. In desperation, I liquidated our IRA accounts and sold the few gold coins I had just to keep the business going. Every morning at four a.m., I drove across the San Francisco Bay to deliver bagels for five hours before opening the store so that we would have some spendable income. When I had to leave this part-time job due to exhaustion, we had no real personal income, for every penny the store earned had to go to pay bills or buy new inventory. When I applied for a bank loan, the loan officer literally laughed in my face. With an infant child and house payments, it seemed our dream was about to become a nightmare. That's when Lee entered our life.

Lee came into the store as a customer, and became one of our best friends. He was tall, strong, and kind. And he was one of the most gentle men I've ever met. Mia and I called him "our angel" because he was incredibly supportive and helpful in those difficult times when we were just getting the business on its feet. When he sensed that we were a little discouraged, he would always have positive words and good solid practical advice to help us out.

If we needed help moving things around, he would always be there. If we needed boxes opened (we still couldn't afford employees) he would cheerfully volunteer. One of his practical suggestions was to give customers a free gift with every purchase. So we started to give little pieces of amethyst, rose quartz or carnelian—even sticks of incense—along with every purchase over ten dollars. Customers loved it and kept coming back. Within a year, we had a flourishing business with a loyal and appreciative clientele.

Until we sold the store to move to Arizona, Lee always seemed to be there when we needed someone to help out. He was truly an angel to us, and his generous spirit and amazingly positive words and suggestions will always be an inspiration. Lee lovingly applied the law of the seed in virtually all he did.

The law of the seed is mastered when we learn how to give. Every gift carries the seed of its fruition, returning ultimately to enrich the one who gives. In order to receive benefits in life, our actions must provide benefits to others. We improve our condition mentally, physically, and spiritually in direct proportion to the manner in which we have assisted those around us. We are the recipients of the forces we ourselves originate in the stream of life. The more we give of all that is good, the more of all that is good will flow into our lives. Ultimately, we give to ourselves and we withhold from ourselves. Suffering is self-inflicted, happiness is self-bestowed.

The law of causation is the law of reciprocal action. This law works in our favor when we acquire the attitude and habit of giving. Giving is the happy habit, the victorious addiction that sets us free. In the game of life, givers win and takers lose. The hand that gives, gains. The winning strategy is the generous strategy.

As a consequence of this fundamental law of life, it follows that our environment and affairs are the result of the sum of our givingness throughout all the years of our existence. Those who take more than they give are living on borrowed time. Eventually the piper must be paid. It may appear that the selfish and deceitful prosper while the industrious and generous fail to make progress. But this is a temporary condition. Eventually, all must experience the consequences of their actions. The surest way to improve the conditions of your celestial bank account is to give. You get out of the red by giving more than you take, and by giving only that which is good, beneficial, helpful and kind. No giving can go unrewarded. In time, you will reap a bountiful harvest, for giving opens the floodgates of receiving.

Many people have an intellectual comprehension of this law of sowing and reaping. But for this understanding to work its transforming magic we must absorb it in our hearts and express it in actions. I once knew two women, both in their sixties, who had shared a house together for many years. Both of them were gifted professionals and had studied spiritual teachings for decades. In most respects they were intelligent, capable, and idealistic. Yet they had a blind spot, it seemed, for in their behavior toward each other they were often atrocious. Between themselves they could be petty, mean-spirited and argumentative. Each was highly critical of the other—face to face and behind each other's back. I knew them well enough to know that they both espoused firm belief in the law of causation, yet for some reason they were unable to live it in their relationship with each other.

Living the law of the seed requires discernment in our thoughts so that we anticipate the consequences of our behavior before we act. "In every affair," warned the Greek philosopher, Epictetus, "consider what precedes and what follows." East

Indian mythology illustrates this pictorially. Saraswati, the beautiful goddess of wisdom, is often accompanied by a swan. According to tradition, the swan is able to separate milk from water as she drinks from a bowl containing both liquids. This represents the faculty of discrimination in action—perceiving in advance the consequences of our deeds—one of the hallmarks of enlightened living. By exercising discernment, we can plow the fields of life wisely, and plant seeds that bring a joyful harvest. If not, we may all too often "sow the wind and reap the whirlwind."

So many people reach the point where they stop making progress in their lives. They begin to atrophy, harden and die. All this could change if they began to give. It does not matter what your current position or circumstance may be. Giving releases a magic, healing power which—due to the inevitable reciprocity at the heart of all action—eventually returns to benefit the one who gives.

A knowledge of this basic life truth is a tremendous power. But it would be a mistake to approach the practice of giving as a kind of "bargaining with God." Charitableness that is egotistical in nature—that is prompted by a desire to appear superior or to curry favor—is tainted and devalued. To make a spectacle of giving—or using it as an attempt to bribe people or buy favors—is to diminish the good that comes from it. Giving that is manipulative or that has strings attached is not true giving. The less egotism in generosity the better. The famous Greek Cypriot healer known as Daskalos suggested that whenever possible, giving should be done anonymously.

Just to be sure readers don't misunderstand this concept, giving does not mean becoming emotionally or physically drained, sacrificing time that you really need for yourself, or being somebody's doormat. It is not a call for martyrdom or overnight saint-hood. The impressive literature that has grown up around the issue of codependency provides eloquent testimony that there is a wrong way to give. What is emphasized here is a primordial fact of nature—an existential law established not by human caprice—but by divine authority. When we act, the universe reacts. As we give, the universe gives back. If my life is less than satisfactory, to find the cure I need only look in the mirror.

Breathing is nature's image of a healthy approach to the concept of giving. Just as the lungs cannot always expel air, but have to inhale after each outbreath, so do we need to know when to seek our own restoration and renewal. If the atmosphere—the air and sky—did not draw water from the oceans and the soil through evaporation, it would have no rain to give back to the earth.

Times of recreation and personal renewal are essential if we are to have anything worthwhile to offer others. We need to know when to take care of ourselves. One of life's greatest pleasures is to be able to enjoy solitude. Solitude and quiet time are necessary if we are to have strength for life and for giving.

In many ways the most important gift we can bring to others is the effort we make to improve ourselves. "If the rose adorns itself," wrote the great poet, Goethe," does it not also adorn the garden?" Self-education and personal development are the foundation for the expression of service. We cannot remove dirt from someone else's eye if our own hands are soiled. To heal and help others, we must first heal and help ourselves.

Giving doesn't just mean giving material things, of course. Often the most valuable gifts are much more subtle. The mother who lovingly teaches her child how to make something, the father who plays wholeheartedly with his children, the teacher who passes on a skill, or the stranger who dispels the shadow of depression with a funny or inspiring tale; these are gifts of measureless value. A kind word or a helpful thought may be of far greater significance than a monetary or material gift. The point is that everyone can give something, even if it only be their prayers, which in the end may be the most valuable gift of all.

People who find themselves alone and unhappy can turn their lives and fortunes around if they understand this basic principle. Those who have something useful to offer, who can give of themselves, will always be appreciated. One of the most charming and well-liked people I know is a woman named Marie, who never goes anywhere empty-handed. She is always writing cheerful cards, giving gifts or flowers, or taking fresh baked goods to her friends and acquaintances. Marie gives spontaneously and lovingly, not because she hopes to receive something in return, but because she loves to make other people happy. She exemplifies the highest attitude in giving: that we give not with personal gain in mind, but as a spontaneous outpouring of the heart. As a result of her loving and generous approach to life, Marie's own life is full of love. She has mastered the secret of the seed, the power of giving.

Another remarkable characteristic of the law of causation is that the forces we set in motion by our gestures develop a mysterious momentum all their own. We do not know where they will end. The universal fabric of life is a seamless tapestry and the effects we originate by our actions extend outward in all directions, much as a pebble tossed into a pond creates widening ripples. We might think of this as the "domino effect" of all action. Our deeds in life have consequences far beyond those of which we become aware.

When camping in the mountains with his students, the Bulgarian mystic and saint, Peter Deunov, would tell them to pour water on a stone or plant—for no apparent reason. In this way he tried to make them aware that even seemingly insignificant gestures have ongoing effects and far-reaching influences—that everything in the subtle web of life is interconnected. Modern physics calls this web of life the "unified field." We are all creating ripples in the same "pond."

To comprehend the full significance of the law of the seed, we must realize that our thoughts and feelings are as real and enduring as any physical action. Not only what we *do*, but *who we are* is constantly setting forces in motion that return to us in the form of experiences, circumstances, and conditions. To grasp this fact, we must come to realize that our physical body is only a fraction of our total self. Our personality manifests through a web of feelings, thoughts, and emanations that create a force field around us—what is often called our personal "energy field," or aura. The nature of our emanations—the full spectrum of one's inner life and external actions at any given time—sets up a "resonance" that stimulates a sympathetic response from the universal life in which we are imbedded. In other words, our consciousness at any moment elicits a vibratory response or current from the larger life in which we live. This current flows into our lives as a sense of well-being or otherwise, depending on the quality of the force we emanate from our thoughts and moods. We give out constantly, not only through physical gestures and the performance of "service," but by every impulse of our inner lives. This may be a difficult idea to grasp at first, but it will become clearer as we unfold our explanations of the universal laws.

The path to happiness and freedom begins with a comprehension of the just law of causation—the law of the seed. When we give, naturally and spontaneously—becoming benefactors to all of life—our own life will be gradually transformed for the better. Each helpful, generous action becomes a seed planted in the garden of our personal well-being. In time, we will be astonished and delighted at the harvest of abundance that comes streaming into our personal world.

In the age to come, to be miserly, greedy or selfish will be seen as a form of illness which blocks the circulatory flow of abundance into our lives. Giving will become a science and an art. In the words of Hilda Charlton, "A life is worthless that does not reach out a helping hand to others." Your power to give is your greatest power.

Perhaps life's greatest secret is that each of us is an immortal spirit-seed manifesting itself through physical life. Our spirit self is the dynamic seed-potential of our being. We unfold the potential of our spirit—the universal spiritual spark within us—through action in life. The motivating principle at the heart of the spirit-seed is desire. The essence of this desire is love. As we manifest love through our actions, we come to know that our essential nature, the seed of our spirit, is love itself. By expressing love in our actions and our thoughts, we gradually come to know the truth of our being—that we are love.

Apply the law of the seed in all your circumstances and set in motion the wheels of a better life. Become a giver and you will be crowned the master of your destiny.

*******

**Polishing the Jewel: Releasing the Magic of the Seed.**

Activity # one
For one week perform the following experiment: Every day think of at least a half dozen actions that you can perform that will enhance your own and other people's lives. These can be any constructive deed: writing a cheerful letter, cleaning out closets and giving charitable donations of clothes you no longer need or use, surprising a friend with a gift, taking someone to lunch, smiling at all the children you see. Keep a record of your sowing. Make a note of each "seed." Consider them as deposits in your heavenly treasury, the balance of which will determine your future circumstances. Get into the habit of releasing constructive currents into the ocean of life. Give those you meet a "flower," even if it be only in the form of a kind thought. Remember that thoughts, words and feelings are also seeds. Become a benefactor to those you contact. Begin now to recreate the garden of your life; transform your future by applying the magic of the seed.

Activity # two
Think of something that you have always dreamed of doing, but for some reason never have. Perhaps it is visiting Europe, spending a week in Acapulco, or taking a voyage on a cruise ship. Or perhaps you've been meaning to enroll in an art or drama class at the junior college, go on a wilderness visionquest, or climb a nearby mountain. Make a commitment to doing something that will bring you pleasure and expand you as a person. Think of it as a gift of love to yourself. Remember that as we become more generous in our lives, we expand our own consciousness of deserving.

Affirmations

*"Giving opens the way for receiving. I master the law of the seed by giving constructively to all who can benefit by my actions."*

*"I transform my life into a beautiful garden by sowing positive seeds each day."*

*"The more I give to others of that which is beneficial and helpful, the more I will receive."*

# CHAPTER TWO
# The Second Jewel — The Magic of Thinking

*"What a man thinketh, that is he; this is the eternal mystery...Man becomes that which he thinks."* — The Upanishads

*"There is nothing fashioned by man that is not first fashioned by his thoughts."*
— Joan Grant, *Winged Pharaoh*

*"Thoughts held in mind, produce after their kind."*
— Charles Fillmore

*"Nurture your mind with great thoughts."* — Benjamin Disraeli

*"Everything interpenetrates everything else."*
— Dr. David Bohm

"I am not all contained between my hat and my boots," wrote Walt Whitman, expressing his conviction that the source of his consciousness and power was within his deeper self—of which his physical body was the outer expression. The poet's intuition has now been confirmed by modern science. In the words of Max

Planck, the famed physicist, "Mind is the matrix of all matter." His statement supports one of the fundamental assertions of the ancient wisdom teachings—all things in the universe have been shaped by mind.

One of the great discoveries of the new science is that human beings do not stand outside of nature as some kind of uninvolved observers. According to the famous *Heisenberg Principle* of quantum physics, our observation of events *influences* those events. We are not spectators at the ballpark, we are playing in the game. Ours is a participatory universe. We participate by our very presence and perception. The activity of our minds creates circumstances. Awareness is power.

The origin of human experience is in one's consciousness. It is absolutely essential to grasp this fact. Your inner world of thought and feeling creates your outer world of environment and relationship. The nature of your thoughts will determine the kind of experiences you draw to yourself.

Even a little reflection will show that our inner, subjective world of thought and attitude conditions our perception of life and events. Take the example of four people hiking together in a forest. One is completely absorbed in personal problems; all he can think about is a recent argument with his girlfriend. He barely notices the forest at all. Another constantly complains about the dampness, the insects, the possibility of wild animals; for her it is a miserable experience. A third hiker observes the trees and speculates to himself the number of board feet of lumber in each, and how much profit could be made by logging the forest for timber. The last companion in the group is absorbed in poetic admiration of the magnificent plants and vegetation. She is transported into a reverie of wonder and admiration at nature's splendor—awed by the vista of teeming life. The experience of each hiker is the result of his or her inner life of consciousness. Hence the saying of Hari Das Baba: "If you meet a thief, he will see only your pockets."

Socrates, the great Athenian philosopher, said that "The unexamined life is not worth living." Self-knowledge begins as we become conscious of our inner lives. The first step on the road to enlightenment is to become aware of the thoughts that pass through our minds. This enables us to gain control of our thoughts, focusing on the positive and constructive ones. The process of personal growth and life improvement originates in the awareness of our thoughts and feelings—the building materials of life.

The next step is to take hold of our inner world of thoughts. The law of the seed applies in the realm of thinking. Our minds are a fertile garden and each thought is a seed. A seed thought takes root and begins to sprout, grow, and eventually produce fruit of its own kind. A successful gardener is selective in her use of seeds. We can create an inner garden of beautiful roses, or a field of worthless weeds that choke out the sunlight. Ultimately, our life is shaped by our mind.

I knew a young man named Russ who had done some things in his early twenties that had landed him in prison. During the time he was incarcerated he was sent some books that described the power of thought to create one's experiences. Russ was profoundly influenced by what he read. In those months alone in his prison cell he analyzed himself and meditated deeply on the kind of person he would like to become. He left prison a changed man. Russ became an unusually kind, loving, and positive individual who never tired of talking about the spiritual influence of good, constructive thought. He had transformed himself by the renew-al of his mind. Through the influence of inspired thoughts we can remake ourselves in the image of our thinking.

Lily was in her late forties when she discovered the truth that thoughts were the blueprint of life. She had been an unwed teenage mother in a small town during an era when there was great social stigma attached. Consequently, she became socially ostracized and gave up her child for adoption. Suffering from dis-mally low self-esteem, she went through a series of relationships and marriages which ended unhappily. Seeking spiritual help, she visited many churches and was counseled by numerous clergy-men. Although assured by a priest that "God doesn't make junk," she had difficulty believing it applied to her.

For years Lily suffered from chronic illness. In her mid-forties her third husband moved out, leaving her sick, troubled, and dis-consolate. The awakening came for her when she met an older woman, a healer and herbalist who was part Cherokee. Lily stud-ied herbal healing with the woman and her health improved grad-ually. But she continued to hold a grudge against life for all the hardships she had endured. The old healer told her that she would have to change her attitudes about herself and about life if she wanted to completely heal and "start life afresh." Lily began to record her thoughts and beliefs and kept a journal for writing ideas which inspired her. Her knowledge of herbal remedies steadily increased and she began leading nature walks to identify and gather edible plants and healing herbs. Her opinion of herself improved dramatically as she saw how others appreciated the way she shared what she was learning. She became interested in traveling, something she had never done, and began visiting some of the world's sacred sites. She became so enthusiastic that she helped organize several tour groups to visit these sites. Lily discovered that thought is the dynamic force which shapes the experience of life, and that the source of enthusiasm and inspiration is in the ideas she holds in her mind.

An exact explanation of how the mind shapes substance is beyond the scope of this book. The essential thing is to acknowledge that it does. A striking image of this process comes from Indian mythology. The god Vishnu is asked by Indra, the King of the gods, to create a potion that will grant eternal life. Vishnu sets about stirring up the vast Ocean of Milk. Out of the milk come all manner of marvelous creations—extraordinary gems, an elephant, a wish-fulfilling tree and cow, a magnificent white horse. Finally the beautiful goddess, Lakshmi, emerges—created from Vishnu's churning of the cosmic ocean. Lakshmi becomes Vishnu's consort, and the two are virtually inseparable.

Milk is a symbol of the life force. The Ocean of Milk is the universal etheric sea out of which manifest existence springs. Vishnu's churning of the ocean represents the process of thinking and imagination. Out of this activity come material forms. The eventual result of right thinking is the birth of wisdom within us—represented by the goddess Lakshmi. The marriage of love and wisdom—of Vishnu and Lakshmi—leads to eternal life.

Although this mythological imagery deals with gods and goddesses—beings of the divine world—the same principles of creation apply in our lives also. When you think, you "churn" the subtle "ocean of existence," creating "divinities" or "monsters," depending upon the nature of your thoughts. Thus, your thinking is the point of origin for what comes into your life. If your thoughts are positive, they will produce positive, beneficial effects. In other words, if you think wisely and lovingly, you will constantly create your own miracles. You will be fashioning the conditions in your mind for a life on earth of happiness, fulfillment and love. When you have learned to control your thinking, you will find that everything else starts to fall into place.

Mind is the universal womb that gives birth to all material forms. Thus, you cannot escape the consequences of your thoughts and feelings. There is an unbreakable connection—an indivisible link—between your inner world and your outer world. Ultimately, your environment is an image, or reflection, of your mental activity. All of us live in circumstances we have created for ourselves.

The mind is a lens through which we focus the remarkable power of our intentions and our dreams. The stronger and clearer our focus, the more rapidly do we achieve what we seek. The offspring of your inner contemplations will be your deeds. Each individual shapes his life by his thoughts, just as a sculptor shapes the clay into the image he holds in his mind.

Perhaps there is no force on earth greater than a strong intention that is backed by intense mental focus. A time-honored method of goal-achievement is to write down your intentions and read them aloud every day, taking practical steps to reach those goals. The longer you hold an intention in the mind, the more powerful it becomes. If you are sincere enough, eventually the opportunity will arise to accomplish the goal.

When Mia and I decided we wanted to start a book and gift shop, we wrote down in detail our goals. At the time, we were both teachers and had neither the time nor the money with which to realize our intention. But we knew that one day the dream would materialize if we wrote down our goal and focused our thoughts upon it. We created a "book of dreams" and we called our plan, "Project Omega." We wrote a declaration, or mission statement, which captured what we wanted our shop to be like. And we envisioned the kind of storefront we would like to have. I bought several copies of my favorite books and placed then in a special place. This was the beginning inventory of our store. The books were the starter seeds for our "garden."

Years later we were living in another town. Project Omega still seemed an impossible dream. One day Mia drove past a dress shop on a side street near the commercial center. The dress shop was located in a building that seemed to her ideal for a book and gift shop. She took me to see it and I agreed that the dress shop was located in a perfect place. "This or something better," we affirmed together.

Over a year later I was driving in town doing errands. To my dismay, I could not find a parking place near my destination, a street where there was usually abundant parking. Muttering under my breath at the odd circumstance, I finally had to turn down a side street five blocks away. As I got out of the car, I realized I had parked in front of the dress shop we'd visited the previous year. I noticed a sign that said "going out for business sale." Curious, I entered the shop and spoke to the owner, a charming woman from South America. She told me that they were, in fact, going out of business. My heart leaped in expectation, realizing this was the opportunity we'd waited for.

I drove home and told Mia. Our daughter was only six weeks old, but we agreed this was our chance. We said a prayer and decided to take instant action. I called the landlord and met him that very day. Although we had very little capital and no prior business experience, our energy and enthusiasm apparently convinced the landlord to take a risk and we signed a three-year lease. Our intention had become a reality.

Thoughts are really living things. Our thoughts take wing and become forces that draw to us conditions that are in accord with their nature. When you fashion an idea, you give birth to a child on the plane of thought. Over time, one's thoughts crystallize into character and circumstance. We become what we think. Because all physical manifestations are the result of thought, it follows that by working with these ideas we can begin to mold the kind of life we desire. If you think constructively, you will create your own miracles.

Manuel was forty-five years old and unhappy in his work as a Spanish-speaking translator on the east coast. He spent a lot of time brooding, and although he loved his family, would often explode into angry tirades at home. A friend invited him to a seminar on personal growth and empowerment, and he began to apply the principles of universal law. Manuel purchased a quantity of "self-help" books and read them voraciously. He copied inspiring passages out by hand and spent hours studying and affirming the truths he discovered.

One summer he went with a friend on a Church picnic. Before the softball game that was the highlight of the occasion, Manuel sneaked off into the Church and sat quietly in a rear pew, reflecting. The pastor noticed him as he left the building, and a few minutes later they met at the softball game. The pastor of the Church was also the dean of a small religious college. He was so impressed with him that he offered him a position as instructor of Spanish, even though Manuel had no previous experience as a teacher. Manuel accepted and spent the summer preparing to teach introductory Spanish to freshman.

Manuel worked diligently at his new position. Students

appreciated his warmth and friendliness. He offered his services as a tutor in the afternoons, and eventually became an academic advisor. He was one of the most popular instructors on campus. He decided to continue his own education at the college level and soon obtained a masters degree in psychology. Manuel remained in his late-blossoming career for years, always one of the most popular and respected teachers. His life transformation was made possible by the changes he wrought in his mental attitude. As Napoleon Hill said in his famous book, *Think and Grow Rich*, the one thing over which everyone has control is their mental attitude.

Thought is the greatest power in life, for it determines the direction we take. We live in a sea of energies—a universe of forces and frequencies of almost infinite variety. We benefit ourselves by being selective in what we choose to focus our attention. Thoughts may be conceived as wave forms or frequencies, analogous to radio and TV waves, but much more subtle. Our minds are like radio receivers and may be attuned to many and varied frequencies. Not only do we constantly receive thoughts with our minds, but we broadcast them as well. Though it may be difficult to imagine, the activity of your mind has an influence that reaches to the farthest star.

Because many people are mentally attuned to that which is discordant, ugly and chaotic, their lives mirror these characteristics. If you choose, you can become instead a receiving station for the angelic vibrations of harmony, concord, and happiness. Mental attention is your tuning device—the focal point of consciousness. Good, positive, loving thoughts have a very high frequency. When you tune your instrument to receive the frequencies of healing, positivity and love, you become a broadcasting station for that which is luminous and helpful. Your own life will gradually reflect these qualities. By focusing attention on thoughts that embody the qualities we seek, we develop those qualities in our personalities.

Once we realize the indestructible link between our inner world of thought and our outer world of experience, we realize that no one is a victim of circumstance. We create our circumstances by the thoughts we entertain, habitually and persistently. We bring into being that on which we focus our attention. When we concentrate upon a particular scenario, we give life and reality to the very images we picture.

Even one's physical body is a creation of thought. Your body is a hieroglyph or image of your consciousness. Our bodies, in their good or ill health, will reflect the thoughts upon which we habitually dwell. One's features reveal character, the inner life of soul. The higher the frequencies of thought and feeling which we create in our minds, the more perfect will be our physical well-being.

It may be true, as some quantum physicists have suggested, that the human body itself is a projected image, a holographic picture, created by our thinking spirit. Perhaps the brain is a kind of screen upon which the mind projects images. It may be that each of us first existed as an image in the mind of God. Regardless of what the science of the future may reveal to us about our origin and destiny, you can gain command of your life right now by controlling your mind.

One of the most wonderful attributes of the mind is the power of imagination. This is a truly magical instrument in our repertoire of life-building tools. So little is really understood about this power. Yet it is unbelievably great. The secret of creation lies in the imaging faculty of the mind. Imagination is the key to creativity. When you visualize a scene or a picture in your mind's eye, you are forming images out of the substance of your soul. In time, these pictures will crystallize into actual physical realities. In this manner we fashion the world in which we live. In reality we shape two worlds, first our inner soul life, and as a consequence, our material circumstances. These two are intimately related, for environment is the reflection of our inner world of consciousness. Our material surroundings mirror our minds, and are the externalization of our inner life.

The human mind's ability to think pictorially and symbolically is a doorway to a subtle form of intelligence. Psychology recognizes that our dreams are a form of communication from the deeper, unconscious part of our selves. Dreams are the picture language of the soul, by means of which the subconscious and superconscious levels of mind communicate their wisdom to our conscious, "awake" mind. Dream interpretation reveals a wealth of information of which our everyday consciousness is generally unaware.

The power of imagination—of pictorial thinking—to develop genius and reveal truth was recognized by Albert Einstein. When asked how to educate so as to produce intelligent children, he responded, "Tell them fairy tales." When asked how to produce *really* intelligent children, he replied, "Tell them *more* fairy tales."

It is significant that much of the traditional wisdom of the human race has been stored up in the form of the imaginative stories we know as mythology, legend, and parable. "It would not be too much to say," writes Joseph Campbell, the modern popularizer of the wisdom in folklore, "that myth is the secret opening through which the inexhaustible energies of the cosmos pour into human cultural manifestation."

Consider an example from Greek mythology—the story of Ariadne's golden thread. Ariadne is the daughter of King Minos, the ruler of Crete. Under the palace of King Minos is a famous labyrinth wherein dwells a Minotaur, a monstrous creature—half man, half bull. No one who enters the labyrinth comes out alive. Theseus, the heroic son of the king of Athens, volunteers to go into the labyrinth, courting certain death.

On his way into the dark maze, Ariadne, who loves Theseus, gives him a ball of golden thread. Theseus ties the thread to the door of the entrance into the labyrinth, then unwinds it as he makes his way through the underground passageways. He finally meets the dreaded Minotaur and slays the beast in hand-to-hand combat. Theseus finds his way back through the confusing maze thanks to Ariadne's golden thread. Theseus and Ariadne then depart for Athens to be married.

Theseus represents the human individuality—the divine spark—that must find its way through the confusing labyrinth of earthly experiences. The Minotaur represents the many dangers in life that would destroy us. In particular, it represents the soul-destroying influence of materialism—ignorance of the spiritual laws that govern life. The ball of golden thread represents the light of wisdom that emanates from our soul, or Higher Self, symbolized by Ariadne. This ancient story teaches us through its imaginative pictures that we must discover the golden thread of wisdom in order to find our way in life. That thread of wisdom comes from our deeper self, which radiates the light and love that guide us.

Stories like Ariadne's Golden Thread depict the intuitive wisdom that comes through inspired fantasy and mythic imagination.

The great mythologies of the world are the "dream images" of the human race. Myths are the soul of humanity speaking to us out of its wisdom-filled depths. Myths and parables convey truth on multiple levels and always have more than one valid interpretation. Allegorical stories such as traditional fairy tales convey truths that will speak to an assortment of listeners with varying degrees of spiritual and intellectual sophistication. Mythic imagery provides spiritual nourishment for all, regardless of one's stage of inner readiness, while revealing a deeper message for those wise enough to comprehend.

All of this suggests that our imagination has immense importance for our spiritual lives. Sages have taught that through the wise use of imagination, in periods of meditation and prayer, we may gradually become aware of higher spiritual dimensions that are interwoven with the physical earthly life. According to the sacred literature of the world's wisdom traditions, at the time of death the soul departs the physical body and becomes conscious in these higher dimensions. The soul finds itself in the higher ethers surrounded by its own thought creations. Thus, we are drawn in the afterlife to the "levels" of universal vibratory substance that correspond to our dominant trend of mind while on earth.

By cultivating a healthy imagination we can begin to unlock the deeper mysteries of life—the *meaning* within our experiences. This ability to discern meaning leads to the development of intuition and inspiration. Imagination is a key which can open the gates of the celestial worlds. With it, one can unlock the hidden powers of the soul and the mind. The developing of an imaginative consciousness is a step towards the unfolding of wisdom in our lives. We can build a light-filled future for ourselves—and those whose lives we touch—by the luminous weavings we create in our imaginations now.

We begin to revolutionize our experience when we acknowledge that thought is the most dynamic power in shaping our life. It is true that our deeper self—our indwelling spirit presence—is pure joy, bliss, and love beyond any concept of the mind. But we can only build a bridge to our immortal spark through enlightened mental activity. The mind is an instrument of incalculable power.

Your circumstances tomorrow will be a reflection of your thoughts today. Life is essentially a process that is set in motion by the dynamo of thinking. Each person's life is a mirror of his or her mental activity. Those who think great thoughts will accomplish great things. You can never be greater or better than your thoughts. The Hunas—native shamans of Hawaii—have an expression that captures the right attitude in regard to thinking about one's life. "Bless the present. Trust yourself. Expect the best."

Your life can become a garden of love and happiness if you fill your mind with kind and light-filled thoughts. In time, you will find that the physical environment in which you live will reflect the garden you have created within. Begin now to transform your life by the transformation and renewal of your mind.

\* \* \* \* \* \* \*

**Polishing the Jewel: Releasing the Magic of Thinking**

Activity # one

Perform the following experiment: For one week go on a "mental diet." Allow yourself to think only positive thoughts. Negative thoughts will come to your awareness, but resist them by replacing them with positive, constructive thoughts. Keep a record of your success. If you think negatively, begin again on day one. When you can go a week with only positive thoughts, you will have taken a giant stride in transforming your life.

Activity # two

Many people are surprised to learn that observation of one's surroundings is a great way to sharpen the mind. During the course of the day, be *mindful* of what you see in your environment. Notice what people are wearing—their shoes, the colors and style of their clothing. Pay attention to the nuances of their speech. Wherever you go, look carefully at your surroundings. Notice the details of color, architecture, and furnishings.

At the end of the day take five or ten minutes and recall in your mind the details of what you observed. If you can't remember particulars—such as the color of the woman's sweater just ahead of you in the supermarket checkout line—then imagine a color. It's all right to fill in the details for what you can't fully recollect. This exercise creates mental alertness. It is helpful in developing memory, as well as enhancing moment by moment awareness during the day. (A note of caution: be careful not to judge people critically according to dress, speech, etc. The purpose here is simply to sharpen observations skills and thereby sharpen your mind.)

<u>Activity # three</u>

Make a list of at least five thoughts or affirmations that embody qualities you would like to develop more strongly— virtues or strengths you would like to express in your life. They may be thoughts you find in this book, read elsewhere, or that you composed yourself. They should have meaning and importance to you.

Read these thoughts aloud until you have committed them to memory. Affirm them silently in your mind each day as often as you can. These thoughts are seeds that will eventually blossom into features of character. It is important to think these thoughts, with intensity and feeling, at least once every day.

## Affirmations

*"I transform myself by the renewal of my mind. I fashion my mind into a temple of wisdom and truth."*

*"All my thoughts are positive, loving and light-filled. I create a better life for myself now by my bright and luminous thinking."*

*"My mind is a fountain of understanding, blessing and enlightenment."*

*"My thoughts are inspired, considerate and helpful. I transform my mind into a garden of beauty and success and my life reflects this transformation."*

# CHAPTER THREE
## The Third Jewel — The Magic of Feeling and Desire

*"Great is my joy when you ask from your heart."* —
Anonymous, *Turning*

*"The fragrance of the flowers is their prayer."* — Peter Deunov

If you ask people to point to themselves, they will almost always point to their heart, almost never their head. A great truth is revealed by this gesture. Although the wellspring of consciousness is in our thinking process, the mystery of our soul—our deeper identity—is bound up with our feelings. It is true that our life is shaped initially by our minds. But it is our feelings and our desires that give life and energy to our thoughts. Feelings bring our thoughts down to earth and provide the spark of motivation. Without feelings, life would be dull, bland and lifeless.

Thoughts are a subtle frequency far removed from the densities of material substance. The bridge between ideas and material objects is the world of feelings. Feelings include moods, emotions and desire. It is in the womb of desire that our intentions are conceived. And the mind ever dwells on that which the heart loves.

Desire is the motivating impulse that gives energy to our

thoughts and direction to our imagination. Desire is the spark that ignites our will into action. It is also the fuel that feeds our dreams of what we want to accomplish in life. Feelings compel us to get up and go.

Without feelings, life would be sterile. From this it follows that the most sublime feeling is also life's most compelling element. This element is *love*. Thoughts and feelings of love are the world's irresistible driving force. When you work lovingly and harmoniously with universal law, the entire universe will work with you to help you achieve your good intentions. We will have more to say about the power of love in later chapters.

Some people say that feelings are neither right or wrong, good or bad; they are just feelings. This is true in part, for feelings seem to well up from an unknown fountain, with an irresistible pressure from within us. But it is also important to recognize that emotions are not neutral. Different feelings produce very different effects.

If we get caught up in the small discomforts and petty inconveniences of life, we may find that irritability saps our energy. A facet of living wisely is to discriminate between serious issues and trivial matters. My daughter once gave me some good advice on how to respond to small disturbances. One day when she was seven years old, we were playing "restaurant"—one of her many delightful make-believe games. I sat in a chair at the kitchen table while she pretended she was the waitress at a fine restaurant. As she set a heavily-laden tray on the tablecloth by my place, the glass of water tipped and spilled. With perfect calm and absolute sincerity she said, "Dad, pretend that didn't happen." Benjamin Franklin would have endorsed my daughter's remark. One of his personal life precepts goes as follows: "Be not disturbed at trifles,

or at accidents common or unavoidable." Allowing petty disturbances to get under our skin deflects us from more important
matters and robs us of inner peace.

Perhaps the best analogy to the diversity of human feelings is
the great variety of colors in nature. Goethe, who was a scientist
as well as one of the world's great poets, said that "Colors are the
joys and suffering of the light." The same may be said of our emotions—they reflect the joys, sorrows, and dramas of life. Most of
the time we experience a mixture of feelings. Our emotions are
like a tapestry of colors of every shade and hue.

It is true we must honor our authentic feelings, not deny or
suppress them. They are an immense source of strength. But it is
important to discern between those which lead to a happier life,
and those which hold us back—between emotions which liberate
and those which pull us down. The ultimate work of art is our
own life. In our journey to the light, we can strive to create a rich
palette of vibrant feelings with which to paint the landscape of
our experience. The colors in our palette are our moods and feelings. We can make our life an expression of beauty—a masterpiece that illustrates our path towards enlightenment and self-
realization—if we are careful in the colors we choose.

Discordant emotions—such as those of hatred, envy, greed,
and jealousy—can wreak havoc in one's own and other people's
lives. Many people feel they have the right to express their angry
feelings, regardless of consequences, in the spirit of being open
and direct. This may be better than bottling up negative feelings,
which then become simmering resentment, eventually surfacing
as explosions of rage or as physical illness. But great care must be
taken in expressing our emotions in relationships. Otherwise,
serious harm can be done. It is helpful to keep in mind the law of

the seed, for when harsh words are expressed in moments of anger, we cast forces to the wind that will one day return to the sender. There is a fine line between being open and communicative, thus "clearing the air," and tactlessly expressing volatile emotions. Often we thoughtlessly arouse the furies when we discharge harsh feelings in our relationships. This leads to still more bitter experiences.

There is still an enormous amount to be learned about creative ways of transmuting discordant feelings into positive and creative ones. Popular psychology of today has only begun to explore this area. We know it is useless to deny emotions. And venting harsh feelings such as anger will only cause harm to ourselves and others. Dark emotions show where we have been hurt in our lives. Emotional healing begins when we can go beneath the armor of our hurt feelings and discover our essential nature. We must learn to acknowledge our emotions and recognize that they are signposts which point to our deeper self. Beneath the mask of our wounded feelings shines the light of our true self, whose nature is love.

At the present time, there is a great need for individuals to establish harmony in their feelings and emotions. According to what is often called the Ageless Wisdom—the body of teaching presented in the ancient temples and which is resurfacing today through a multitude of books and teachers—the emotional realm is related to what is known in traditional theology as the Holy Spirit, and is closely connected to the Divine Feminine. Here lies a clue to the path of emotional healing.

In the early days of Christianity, St. Paul taught in the city of Ephesus, located in modern-day Turkey. Ephesus was one of the principal centers of learning in the ancient world. The ancient

Greek Temple of Diana at Ephesus was so spectacular and beautiful that it was considered one of the seven wonders of the world. Although this and other mystery temples were later destroyed, much of the wisdom taught in these schools seeped into early and mediaeval Christianity.

A student of St. Paul, known to history as Dionysius the Areopagite, is credited with writing a book in which was codified in Christian form much of the teaching of the Mystery Schools regarding that class of glorious beings known as angels. Following an ancient precedent that we may presume is based on an actual clairvoyant perception, Dionysius listed nine classes or levels of angels. They range from those luminous spirits which are very close to the lives of human beings, called guardian angels, all the way to the Seraphim angels who stand before the "throne" of the universal powers and ceaselessly chant the holy name of God.

In his writings, St. Paul made reference to the mysterious Order of Melchizedek. The Order of Melchizidek is that group of individuals known in metaphysics as the Masters of Wisdom. In Christianity they are known as the "community of Saints," and in the Hebrew Cabala they are called the *Ishim*, or "perfect men." According to the teaching of the Mystery Schools, which was known to St. Paul, the Order of Melchizidek is that class of human beings just below that of the lowest rank of angel. When Jesus said "be perfect as your father in heaven is perfect," he was instructing human beings to so harmonize their inner and outer lives that they could eventually become a part of the human "hierarchy" of perfected souls, that illustrious group of initiates called by St. Paul, the Order of Melchizidek.

Within this order, there are as many women as there are men. Traditionally, at the highest level of initiation the men are called

Masters of Wisdom and the women are called Daughters of Wisdom, or Daughters of Light. The leader of the Daughters of Light is the heavenly spirit known as the World Mother. This being has many names, including the Divine *Sophia*, in Greek, and *Shekinah*, in Hebrew. The psychologically minded may prefer to think of her as an archetype, but she is in fact a being of the most exalted stature. It may be helpful to picture the Mother of the World as an archangel.

Throughout history there have been many representatives on earth of the Heavenly Mother. At this time in history, she is drawing very close to humanity in a variety of forms, but through one form in particular, at least in the west. I had an experience in which this being became more than merely a concept to me, but a personage of great love, mercy, and tenderness.

Mia and I were living in San Rafael and our book and gift shop was located near the San Rafael Mission, one of the original Spanish missions in California. When I had the chance, I enjoyed sitting quietly in the tiny chapel of the restored mission building. I was not raised Catholic, and Mother Mary was little more to me than an image in Renaissance art. But as I developed my thoughts on the subject, I began to think of her as a representative of the Divine Mother, a human embodiment of the sacred feminine. In my meditation one autumn afternoon in the mission chapel, I prayed to her to make herself known to me. As I left the chapel to return to my store, I grabbed a handful of small pamphlets with her image on the cover and stuffed them into my shirt pocket over my heart.

I was the only one working that evening in our store and I was unusually fatigued. Just before closing, a man came in and hovered around the book cases. He asked me if I could recommend a book to him that would be a good gift for his girl friend. He seemed a little scruffy, but I didn't notice anything about him that would cause me to be on my guard. A few moments later he walked to the counter with the book and set it down, as if ready to make a purchase. I sensed that his mannerisms were strange, but again—perhaps because of fatigue—the intuitive signals I often receive at times of danger didn't register.

He hesitated when I told him the price of the book, and I sensed that he was an "oddball." At that moment he reached into his trouser pocket and drew out a handgun, pointed it at my heart, and with a sinister grin demanded that I give him all the money in the register. I suddenly knew what it meant to "jump out of one's skin." I stepped back in shock, my heart pounding fearfully. I cannot remember ever being so frightened. My first impulse was to give him the money and not provoke him in any way. But despite my fear, I felt a growing sense of outrage at this act of violence against me. In what was probably a very stupid thing to do, I told him that I'd already pressed the emergency alarm button, which notifies the police of a holdup. It was a complete bluff, for we had no such button. The thief might have shot me right then, but instead he walked around the counter and hit me over the head with the butt of his gun. Then he reached into our cash box and began to grab the money. I fell to my knees with the impact of the blow, then stood up beside the man. An incredible power seemed to swell up from within me and took hold of my mind and body. I felt completely superior to and more powerful than the gunman, and my terror, which moments later had been overwhelming, completely vanished. I was filled with a force of absolute righteousness and authority. Grabbing the cash box from the man's hands, I heaved it over the counter onto the floor, money scattering everywhere. At the top of my lungs I shouted at the criminal, ordering him to leave my store.

The gunman hurried around the counter and headed for the door, stooping to snatch a few coins on the way. I chased after him, and on the way out of the store I grabbed, of all things, a crystal ball. I raced down the block into the parking garage and threw the crystal ball at the gunman as he tried to make his escape. I missed and he got away.

A customer who had been the only other person in the store had crawled from her hiding place and called 911. The police arrived within minutes, but the thief was never found. When I came down to earth from the rush of adrenaline, I began to sob. It wasn't so much that I was concerned for my own sake about losing my life—for I have never doubted the immortality of the soul and spirit—but the thought of my three-year-old daughter suddenly becoming fatherless was more than I could bear. I had a strong sense that a presence had protected me through the holdup. Remembering the gun pointed at my heart, I reached instinctively for my shirt pocket. There, over my heart, were the little pamphlets with Mother Mary's image that I had stuffed into my shirt when leaving the mission chapel just hours earlier, moments after my specific prayer request for her to make her presence known to me. I felt certain that she had protected me. And often since that time I have been made aware of her influential presence in my life.

The World Mother, however we may conceive of her, is an actual being who has drawn very close to humanity at this time. One of her main tasks is to assist in the emotional healing of the world. She is not only a *symbol* of the emotional healing that we as individuals must accomplish, she is a living force to assist us in the process.

All human beings have been wounded by earthly life. The resurgence of interest in the feminine divine is part of the great healing taking place in the world. This healing must occur first in our emotions and our feelings before we can heal our relationships and the earth itself. The Divine Mother can be seen as both a source and symbol of the healing force that restores the lost harmony of our souls.

In the great myth of ancient Egypt, the divine Isis restored to life the body of her husband, Osiris, which had been cut into fragments by the wicked Set. This is one of the earliest recorded stories of resurrection, and represents the fact that it is the wisdom of the sacred feminine—love in action—which must heal and re-enliven the wounded spirit. Our souls have been damaged and torn by the materialism of modern life, symbolized in the myth by the evil Set. We revitalize our lives when we begin to heal our wounded emotions.

Whether or not one is disposed by personal temperament to call upon the Mother of the World, all of us must work in our own fashion to heal our emotional selves. This healing begins when we learn to transform feelings from negative to positive. We heal our wounded hearts when we begin to love—despite all the good reasons that our minds can find *not* to love. To heal our souls, we must learn to forgive those who have hurt us. When we forgive, we unite ourselves with an actual healing force within nature.

When we walk in nature, we can perceive two contrary streams at work in all things. One is the stream of decay and death, the other is that of life and growth. The force of gravity is related to the stream of death and decay. There is another force in nature—opposed to gravity—which is associated with the stream of growth and unfolding. One might call it the force of lightness and levity. It is a benign influence that draws the plant sunward and helps a young child to stand upright.

This force of lightness and levity—corresponding to the life-bestowing impulse of advancement and growth—is related to our positive thoughts and feelings, just as gravity is associated with our discordant ones.

Negative emotions are subject to the law of gravity. They pull us down, literally and figuratively, and open us to the destructive processes in nature. Toxic thinking releases toxins in our cells which weaken them, ultimately causing the cells to die. These toxins enter the bloodstream and undermine our bodily resistance and immunity. Destructive frequencies of consciousness undermine our constitution, reduce our resistance, and render us susceptible to illness. Every negatively charged thought and emotion is a blow to the health and integrity of our physical bodies. The temple of the body is damaged by the constant impact of discordant feelings.

Positive emotions lift us toward the light, giving us strength, energy and health. We overcome gravity when we overcome negative thoughts and emotions, replacing them with luminous, positive ones. Feelings of love and enthusiasm are the elixir of life, the universal panacea that leads to health and happiness. When we focus our minds on that which is good, beautiful, and true, we awaken feelings that heal, bless, and prosper.

In order to educate the life of feelings, there is no better teacher than music and art. Many people have changed their lives by falling in love with the music of a great composer. The greatest music has an unparalleled ability to elevate the feelings, producing inspiration and joy. Music has the capacity to heal and transform wounded emotions. Perhaps this is why Beethoven said that people who listened to his music would never need to suffer again.

The cathartic power of music, with its ability to produce soul-stirring emotions, is universally recognized. Music has been known to move an entire people to heroic deeds. Guiseppe Verdi wrote his great opera, *Nabucco*, as a thinly veiled metaphor of the political situation of his beloved Italy, which at the time was controlled largely by foreign powers. This fact was not lost on his compatriots, who were inspired when they heard the memorable lyrics and melodies. Verdi's' music helped unite the Italian people behind the efforts of Garibaldi to bring independence and unity to his country.

Music can transform sorrow into understanding and be an impetus to our growth. "As long as a man can sing," said Peter Deunov, "he can find his way out of sorrow." Elevated and inspired music forms a protective aura around an individual, which influences him or her toward harmonious decisions and actions. The power of music to heal and inspire will be used much more commonly in the enlightened therapies of the future.

Our emotions are closely linked to our memory, and the connection between memory and music has long been recognized. Through the mysterious power of association, certain songs or pieces of music will awaken dormant images of long-forgotten memories. Music conjures imagery and emotion because music is a facet or expression of feeling. Music is feeling made audible.

Feelings are the gateway to the heart; they are the substance of our souls. Feelings give depth to character. People of shallow feeling do not arouse much response in others. People with powerful emotional natures, such as poets, mystics, saints and artists, invariably have a strong impact upon their fellows. In order for thoughts to have a direct impact in the physical affairs of daily life, they need to be linked to strong feelings.

It is also true that thoughts alone, no matter how lofty, no matter how positive, are unable of themselves to create happiness. Our best thoughts must penetrate into the emotional dimension, stimulating and awakening corresponding feelings, before we can experience happiness. Happiness comes to those who awaken love in their hearts. Feelings of affection, kindness, love, and appreciation of beauty are the angels that open the gates of contentment.

The higher emotions of love, compassion, joy, serenity, reverence, wonder and devotion are the passport to a deeper state of consciousness—the awareness that life is a seamless tapestry of interrelationship. The wellsprings of genius lie in the cultivation of these powerful feelings that remain slumbering in most people. Such emotions may be kindled by contemplation of inspired art, or by listening to the works of the great composers, or by love of nature. They may be awakened by great literature, poetry, or by the study of the luminous spiritual teachings of the world. One's feeling response to an inspired thought is as important as the idea. Your best feelings become a bridge into a more generous and exalted state of understanding and wisdom. They are the gateway to a happy, creative and fulfilled life.

We choose our direction in life by that which we introduce into our consciousness. In each moment of life we have a choice. We can express a grievance, or see the positive, hopeful element. We can curse the weeds, or rejoice in the flowers. The choice is ours each moment of every day.

*******

**Polishing the Jewel: Releasing the Magic of Feeling and Desire**

Each day for a week set aside at least five minutes for the following exercise. Find a quiet place where you will not be disturbed. Close your eyes, relax your body and your breathing. Visualize yourself standing beside a beautiful mountain waterfall. See yourself stepping into the crystal cascade of the falls. The water is the perfect temperature for you. Imagine that this water has special healing, rejuvenating properties. All darkness of negative, discordant feeling is being removed by this magical, refreshing cascade. Feel all fatigue and resentment vanishing. All bitterness is washed away in the ceaseless torrent from the falls.

Imagine that entirely new and wonderful feelings are pouring into you. Picture yourself as you were at one of the happiest moments of your life. See yourself smiling. Tell yourself that it is natural to experience happiness. Know that the degree of happiness you experience is a result of your habitual emotions. Your thoughts give birth to your feelings. The waterfall represents the positive current in nature that uplifts, restores and heals. See yourself leaving the waterfall and sitting on a comfortable bench by the falls. Imagine that a sun of warmth is shining in your heart. *Feel* the happiness and smile!

Along with this exercise, notice what you are feeling as often as possible during the day. Try consciously to replace negative feelings with the warmth and light of a higher emotion.

## Affirmations

*"Happiness comes to those with love in their hearts. My path is a path of love."*

*"My feelings are a tremendous power. I honor my true feelings by filling them with the light of wisdom, the warmth of kindness, and the power of truth."*

*"I know that one day all my emotions will be positive and life-bestowing."*

*"I realize that my desires are the fuel that feeds my actions. All my desires are becoming constructive; they are leading me to a happy and fulfilled life."*

*"My life continually gets better. I am happy and fulfilled even now."*

# CHAPTER FOUR
## The Fourth Jewel — The Magic of Action

*"In nothing do men more nearly approach the gods than in doing good to their fellow men."*
— Cicero

*"A man grows most tired by standing still."*
— Chinese proverb

*" ...charity isn't a matter of fine sentiments; it means doing things."*
— St. Therese of Lisieux

*"Do all you can and divine energy will always do the rest; but first, you must do all you can."*
— Peter Rosen

When we first become aware that our inner world of thoughts and feelings is the supreme influence in creating our experience, we may have the tendency to discount the importance of physical activity. But this would be a mistake. No progress in life is possible without action.

Many spiritually-minded people have a deeply held belief

that God will take care of all their needs and they need not exert themselves in any way. I believe that this is a distortion of a profound life truth. It is true that Divine Intelligence will take care of our needs—if we work with it by living in accordance with the universal laws. This means learning to become co-creators, not simply passive "watchers."

There is a gigantic difference between working *with* cosmic intelligence and simply expecting everything to drop in our hands. The vital power in the seeds of the vegetable kingdom originates from cosmic intelligence. But we can only have a garden if we till the soil and plant the seeds. True healers will not claim that they are the source of the healing power. But for this healing energy to work through them they must work cooperatively with it. The healing force that mysteriously repairs a broken bone comes from God, but we must first properly set the bone or risk becoming crippled. The following story excerpted from *Survival Guide for the New Millennium*, by Byron Kirkwood, captures the view of working with Divine Intelligence.

> "There was a man in a house and it was flooding outside. A neighbor came by and said 'we need to evacuate.' The man answered, 'No! God is going to take care of me!' The water continued to rise and the man was forced upstairs. Others came by in a boat and offered to rescue him. He told them, 'No! God is going to take care of me.' Finally the man is up on the roof of his house and a helicopter arrives to offer help. Again the man says, 'No! God is going to take care of me.' Finally the water consumes the man and he drowns.

He goes to heaven and is presented before God. He complains to God, 'I thought you were going to take care of me!' God answers, 'I sent you a neighbor, a boat and a helicopter, what more did you need?'"

The above example illustrates the need for action—for involvement in life. The universe will fulfill our needs and supply us with abundance, but only if we can translate thoughts, dreams, and desires into energetic action. There is simply no substitute for work. Like it or not, no lasting reward comes without diligent effort. No great thing was ever achieved without exertion.

Nonetheless, much wasteful and unessential activity can be eliminated by conscious effort in the realm of thought. The game of golf teaches us the importance of economy of energy—of reducing non-essential efforts. Unlike most games, in golf *less is best*. In order to reduce wasteful activity—to take "strokes off your game"—it is necessary to think through one's goals and devise a strategy which will lead to success. Guidance in life comes from within—from our mind, our heart, our soul, and our thinking spirit. In formulating our plans, it is always helpful to commit goals and objectives to writing. Once a course of action has been decided upon, it's time to "get into the act."

On ancient Egyptian art you can sometimes see the image of the sun with many rays extending to the earth. A remarkable thing about these rays is that they have a hand at each end, in a gesture of blessing. This image has great significance. The sun has always been a symbol of the spirit. The hand represents action—the power of will. One interpretation of the sun with the many hands touching the earth is that thinking must be expressed in deeds. It's not enough to have good ideas, you have to get involved to really make a difference. Real commitment is always expressed by action. It is through our "hands," that is, through our work, that we transform our life. Idealism can only make a practical difference if we *live* it.

The fact that the hands of the solar rays—in the above-described Egyptian image—have a soft, caressing gesture is also significant. It represents the fact that enlightened deeds bestow blessings and assistance. Our actions are best when warmth and light shine through them. You can fulfill your purpose and your destiny only if you give fully of yourself.

From where do we draw the inner strength to act? Emerson said, "Do the deed and you shall have the power." Just as no one can eat for you, so no one can perform the deeds that you alone can perform. Each of us is the miracle-working power in all that we desire to have done. The capacity for dynamic action springs from the inner reservoir of our soul. The springboard of action lies in the feelings and desires which prompt us to be up and doing. The more powerful and intense our desires, longings and aspirations—one might say "our dreams"—the more powerful will be our capacity to act. Intention is the seed that gives birth to the deed.

Stephen Jobs, the legendary founder of Apple Computer, knew the importance of taking action. As a teenager, Jobs was brilliant and charismatic, but he was unsure of what he wanted to do with his life. In 1974, at the age of nineteen, he journeyed to India in quest of spiritual inspiration and enlightenment. Upon his return to California, he and Stephen Wozniak built pre-assembled computer circuit boards in Jobs' parents' garage. On April 1, 1976 they formed the Apple Computer company and began marketing the Apple I personal computer. Other companies had designed similar systems, but were not making significant efforts to market their product. Steven Jobs realized the extraordinary potential of the new technology. It was a combination of his and Wozniak's innovations, along with their bold and enterprising marketing efforts, that led to Apple's legendary success. Steven Jobs envisioned the possibilities and he acted with swift and sustained enthusiasm.

We reveal ourselves through our work. Through good work, or right action, we allow the law of causation—the law of the seed—to work to our own benefit. Your deeds in the world are a revelation of your inner life. Henry David Thoreau said that, "If one advances confidently in the direction of his dreams, and endeavors to live the life which he has imagined, he will meet with a success unexpected in common hours." To live wisely is to demonstrate a harmony in your thoughts, feelings and activities.

The ultimate test of any philosophy or worldview is how you live your life. The thing that matters most is *not* what you profess to believe, but how you *actually live*. For this reason Gandhi said, "Show me how a man lives; that is his religion."

The sacred literature of the world reminds us that the highest attitude in action is to perform to the best of our ability and not be anxious about results. The results will take care of themselves in their own time. This perspective suggests that it is best not to act out of a desire for the fruits of our labor, but rather to act out of love for the work itself and because it is the right thing to do. This attitude may seem paradoxical, but it can be emotionally liberating and spiritually enlightening.

Truth is revealed through our actions. Not only do actions speak with more eloquence than words, actions reveal the truth of who we are inwardly. Our inner life cannot be hidden. It is exposed for all to the world to see. Our outer conditions and environment are the mirror of what lives in our minds and heart. What you are on the inside is reflected in your deeds, and in what habitually surrounds you on the outside. In the beautiful words of Kahlil Gibran, "Work is love made visible."

Some people seem to think that it is enough to "just be." But our "beingness" will always shine through the actions that are prompted by our deep-seated feelings, wishes and aspirations. Thoughts and feelings that are not expressed in deeds are like works of art that are hidden away in a damp museum cellar. Much of their value is lost. The truth of who we are is revealed in what we do.

Perhaps that is why Jesus considered a hypocrite to be worse than the lowliest of sinners. For to say or pretend one thing and do another is to engage in spiritual deceit. No doubt, the truth will make us free. But truth is not something that the intellect alone can fully grasp. For truth to be known, it must be lived. To grasp higher truths they must be expressed through the heart and through actions. Action reveals character, just as the full-grown plant reveals the nature of the seed. We transform ourselves and break the chains that enslave us by engaging in constructive efforts. The value of life lies in the wise use of each moment. "Holiness," says Mother Teresa, "does not lie in doing great things. It lies in doing little things with great love."

Actions can be as subtle as a look, a glance, or a gesture. Volumes can be spoken through a loving look or a piercing stare. The eyes are truly the windows of the soul and through our eyes we release powerful forces into the world by our gaze and our glance. A hateful stare can be as destructive as a physical blow. I have seen children burst into tears when looked upon derisively.

The legendary "evil eye" was a deliberate glance so full of malice that the "victim" was known to be stricken as if with a material poison. A gesture of the hands, a nod of the head, a sincere smile—all of these are actions that release forces into the world. An approving look can communicate more in an instant than the most eloquent speech. In fact, the word "countenance," which refers to the face, also means "to grant approval."

Many people have an approach to activity that leads to burnout. The eighties were a period of cultural fatigue for a large segment of society. The go-go lifestyle of that era—the "splash, dash and crash" syndrome—is a caricature of right action. Living an active life does not mean running frenetically on all cylinders until we collapse. In fact, when we learn to simplify our lives by eliminating non-essentials, we may find we have masses of time on our hands. Modern media culture, with the all-pervading seduction of advertising, creates an exaggerated pace. So many people are running after an elusive *something* that they believe will fix their lives. Commercial propaganda takes a huge toll on people's emotional and physical well-being—not to mention their finances.

In many ways, our culture contributes to a distorted view of physical action. The Darwinian view that evolution is "the survival of the fittest" has influenced many people to feel that they must "struggle" to obtain things—that work implies stressful, competitive labor. Life *does* require that we exert ourselves, that we put forth our best efforts, but this does not mean that we must necessarily fight or struggle. Consider the activity of heart and lungs. Through the efforts of these organs our blood circulates and we breathe ceaselessly throughout life. Yet the heart and lungs almost never tire. Only in exceptional instances are we forced to push these organs to the point of exhaustion. Even then, their recovery is quick. The activity of the heart and the lungs is virtually effortless because it is *rhythmic*. This gives us a clue to how to live without struggle. There needs to be balance and rhythm in our activities and our lives. We will discuss the place of rhythm in a harmonious life in Chapter Nine. It will suffice here to call attention to the principle of rhythmic alternation of activities, for it is a key to transcending the struggle for existence.

In the desire to avoid stress, some people have lost sight of the fact that activity is often not the cause of stress at all. Frequently, stress is rooted in emotional and subconscious factors connected to procrastination, that is, the *avoidance* of activity. The source of stress in many cases is having *not done* the tasks that need completion. In this event, no amount of bodywork, massage, or "R and R" is going to relieve the stress. There are times when the best form of stress therapy is getting motivated.

It is important to write down in detail our goals and intentions, but we can only realize our aims if we follow up goal-planning with action. The combination of intention with practical effort often produces surprising results. When I left my teaching position, I had almost no money and needed a job. A friend of mine named Robert was painting houses at the time and I asked him if he needed an assistant. He told me that if I could find a house to paint, I would have a job.

That night I wrote out a short "telephone script," which in essence stated that my professional painting company offered excellent service at reasonable prices. We would be in the area the next day, and if the homeowner wanted their house painted we would be happy to make an offer. Then I picked up the phone book, opened to the "B's," and started calling. The third person I called was a building contractor who was just completing a large home in an upscale neighborhood. The house needed painting—inside and out—and he invited me to come by and make a bid. I called Robert and the next day he drove by the house. He made an offer, got hired, and I had a job.

There are two extremes of unbalanced physical activity which hinder the harmonious application of physical effort. The first is a paralysis of will. Despite good intentions, you simply don't do what you have decided upon. The other is engaging in constant and frenetic activity that is almost a way of filling or ignoring an inner emptiness of soul. As to the first extreme, here are two simple exercises that are helpful in strengthening the capacity to get things done:

Each day choose a simple task—an apparently meaningless action—that has no bearing on your conscious professional goals. It must *not* be an essential part of your life, or something you would normally do for personal pleasure. It may even seem slightly ridiculous, for instance, switching the wrist on which you wear your watch, or bending to your knees, as if to lace up your shoes. Other possibilities are standing on a chair, walking up and down the steps (when you don't need to), or opening a window. With regular practice, exercises of this nature serve to strengthen the will, especially if they are done at the same time each day.

Another simple technique is to act upon an idea as soon as it enters your mind, without hesitation. These two exercises will work to strengthen the acting power so that we are more capable of accomplishing our goals in life. An added benefit is that a strong will eventually shows itself in a stronger, healthier and more youthful body.

As to the second extreme, if one is prone to hyperactivity, possibly as compensation for an inner emptiness, it is helpful to set aside short periods once or twice daily, even if for only five minutes. During this time avoid all sensory stimulation, close the eyes and perform a simple exercise in visualization. Picture yourself in a beautiful natural setting, possibly relaxing in a lovely garden, seated on a bench in a majestic forest, or upon a mountain with a magical vista. Envision the scenery in minute detail. If at first this is too difficult, try listening to uplifting music while perceiving yourself achieving some of your most cherished life ambitions.

Many of our activities are based entirely on habit and the expectations of others. It is important to develop the capacity for individual initiative—to decide upon a task and *do it*. Deliberately changing a habit, even one as simple as reducing the time we sit in front of the television, or taking a walk instead of a nap, can be liberating for the will. Each progressive success leads to broader capacities and a stronger will. The capacity for bold, decisive action is a characteristic of successful people. It may take considerable courage to overcome habitual inertia and do something new and vital, but the results may be electrifying. The famous words of Goethe capture like no other the extraordinary nature of the acting power.

"Whatever you can do or
Dream you can, begin it.
Boldness has genius,
Power and magic in it."

Many people become discouraged by disappointments. These experiences sap their will and their desire to "try again." But failure isn't falling down; it's not getting up. Really, there is no such thing as failure, so long as we continue to learn. We can only learn through being involved with life.

Thomas Edison understood the importance of persistent effort. He is known as a man of genius. He himself said that his discoveries were the result of hard work—"one percent inspiration, ninety-nine percent perspiration." He once told a colleague that during his experiments with electricity, he failed in one experiment more than eighty-one times before finding the right combination of factors which led to success. His colleague was amazed at his perseverance, and exclaimed that it must be like hitting one's head against a brick wall. "Not at all," Edison answered. "You speak of actions that would be painful. I think of challenging excitement. You must see that I always believe I will be successful on the next experiment."

We may not aspire to be inventors, but we can all learn from Edison's perseverance. In pursuing our goals and dreams in life, it's always too early to stop. Perseverance is a master key that eventually proves irresistible. It has been said that "persistence alone is omnipotent."

Through action you meet your destiny. By giving fully of yourself you fulfill your purpose in life. Life cannot be deeply experienced, nor can we develop properly, unless we act. Only through action are we really involved in our own life. Our inner life of soul is awakened through contact with the world.

Without the possibility of testing ourselves in the arena of life, we have no real way of measuring our progress. Almost anyone can be gentle if they live in a remote cave, avoiding contact with other people. The measure of our growth is the manner in which we respond to challenges and difficulties. The specific nature of the events and incidents which come to try us is of secondary importance. How we respond to events is the primary issue—and the test of our maturity.

Ultimately, the most powerful stimulus to action lies in our emotions and desires. By focusing on what we want in our life, we stir our inner life of feelings and this triggers our will. Action is essential to growth, for it is through our experiences among people that we learn the lessons of life and give expression to our aspirations, hopes and yearnings.

Only through deeds can you *live* your dream.

********

### Polishing the Jewel: Releasing the Magic of Action

<u>Activity # one</u>

If you are a former yuppie recovering from "time systemizers," you can probably skip this one. For everyone else, it's a simple and useful tool in getting the most out of life.

Make a "to do" list of daily and weekly goals and objectives. Stretch yourself by including things that aren't easy for you, or for which you have some resistance to doing. Think of it as a game. Make it a challenge. Promise yourself a "prize" if you complete everything on your list. Remember that emotions are the dynamo that sets the will into motion. Try to generate a feeling of enthusiasm for achieving your goals. At the end of each day check off tasks you've completed. Review your weekly list at the end of seven days. Reflect back on your accomplishments. If you've met your goals, celebrate. Give yourself a reward. Treat yourself to something special. If you've failed to meet expectations, make note of your progress and take courage from all that you *did* manage to accomplish. Create a new list for the next week.


Activity # two

For particularly challenging long-term goals it is helpful to create a "book of visions." This can be a notebook, a diary, or a photo album. Create particular affirmations that capture in powerful words what you envision for yourself. Place these in the book along with photographs of yourself in the desired situation, whether it be a new home, a new profession, or perhaps an ideal relationship. See yourself in your mind's eye actually reaching your goals. Visualize the details. How will you feel in the moment of achievement? Imagine yourself in that instant and *feel* that feeling. What would you be thinking? Imagine thinking those thoughts. What clothes might you be wearing? See yourself dressed in them. Picture the surroundings as you imagine they might be.

Remember that at no time should you ever infringe upon the freewill or sovereignty of another person when seeking your personal goals in life. The use of affirmations and visualization in regard to situations that might impose on the freewill of another is, to say the least, unethical, and is to be absolutely avoided.

The feeling that arises from successful completion of goals is one of life's sweetest. It becomes fuel for further achievements. Get in the habit of getting things done and you will become a winner in the game of life.

## Affirmations

*"I am the miracle-working power in everything I desire to have done."*

*"I have a powerful will to achieve."*

*"Every day I get stronger, more decisive, and more effective."*

*"I can accomplish all things through the miracle-working power of the spirit within me."*

# CHAPTER FIVE
# The Fifth Jewel — The Magic of the Spoken Word

*"Words are the dress of thought."* — Samuel Johnson

*"Great words are inspiring. Small words are chatter."*
— Chuang Tsu

*"Out of the abundance of the heart the mouth speaketh."*
— Jesus

The three-pointed crown is an ancient emblem of authority. Although the age of monarchy is over, the symbol of the crown still holds important meaning. It represents *sovereignty*. The word *sovereignty* means "the right to rule." Each human being has that God-given right—the right to govern one's own life—the right to become a free individual.

"One who conquers himself," said Gautama, "is greater than another who conquers a thousand times a thousand men on the battlefield." Every man and woman is meant to exert dominion in their lives. This dominion represents royal authority—kingship and queenship within our personal world. The crown is a symbol of this authority with which we all have been endowed in order to rule supreme over the conditions of our life.

The three points of the crown represent authority and sovereignty in the three "realms" of human life discussed in the previous three chapters: the mind, the emotions, and the physical environment. In traditional metaphysics, the human personality consists of the three "soul forces" of thinking, feeling, and physical will. When we can express dominion in the kingdom of our mind, soul, and physical environment we achieve self-mastery in our lives. No external force can defeat us. The greatest enemies and obstacles are within. Fools and tyrants seek power over others. The wise seek power over themselves.

All human beings have been given a magic wand to help them exert rulership in these three areas or realms of life. It is the tongue—that is, the power of the spoken word. Speech contains a tremendous power for good or for ill. The tongue's twin power, either for benefit or for bane, is seen in the capacity of speech either to bless or to curse. John Templeton tells the following African legend which illustrates the tongue's dual power.

"...an old chief needed to test the wisdom of the young man he had chosen to be his successor as tribal head. He asked the boy to prepare two meals for him. The first meal was to contain the very best ingredients life had to offer; the second meal would contain the very worst.

On the appointed day, the chief sat down to his first meal and it was a delicious plate of sliced cow tongue with vegetables. The chief was delighted with the food and, upon finishing, asked the boy why he had chosen tongue.

'The tongue is one of the finest parts of our being' the

young man replied. 'it can speak wonderful words of truth that can help our people grow and prosper. The right words can give them courage and bolster their integrity. Tongues can speak of love and harmony and hold our village together.'

The chief was very impressed and waited for the second meal with eager anticipation. On the appointed day the chief sat down to eat his second meal and found it to be identical to the first. When he had finished, he asked the boy why he had prepared the same meal twice.

The young man answered, 'The tongue can be the best part of us, but it can also be the worst. The tongue can speak words of anger and discouragement that tear people down and rob them of hope. It can weave deceit; it can speak untruth that causes disharmony. The tongue more than any other weapon can destroy our village life.' The old chief listened closely and nodded his head. He knew he had chosen the next leader wisely."

Our words are forces which are constantly creating our personal world. When we speak, we make our thoughts and feelings audible. Ideas become sound through spoken words. Along with the face value of words—that is, the meaning or thought behind them—speech carries an additional extraordinary power—one that is only beginning to be understood. It is something within the vibratory quality of sound itself.

When I lived in Europe, I had the good fortune to enroll in a school for speech and drama in Switzerland, which was based on the work of the philosopher and educator, Rudolf Steiner. We studied the creative and formative powers of speech—the fact that speech is an expression of our deeper soul. In the ancient temples, the study of the human being's relationship with the cosmos began with the study of speech. While in Switzerland, I discovered the branch of physics called *cymatics*, which has developed in recent years in order to understand the power and influence of sound upon matter. It was pioneered by Dr. Hans Jenny, a Swiss scientist, who coined the term *cymatics* from the Greek word for *wave*. The science of cymatics has demonstrated through laboratory experiments what was known in the ancient Mystery Schools and taught by Pythagoras in his academy in Italy 2600 years ago—that sounds change the very matrix of physical substance itself. Our words literally mold, shape and arrange subtle physical patterns.

Hans Jenny photographed and filmed the effect that different sounds had on various mobile substances, such as powder, water, and sand. His research proves conclusively that sound frequencies create forms in space and substance. Specific sounds create specific forms. These forms are geometric patterns—what might be called "lines of force." Each sound creates its own unique image in space and in substance.

Every time we speak we create vibrational patterns that effect the physical body as well as the atmosphere around us. Although subtle, these sound patterns are as real as the vibrations created by the impact of a hammer on metal or wood. The subtle wave forms we create in space and in our bodies can be compared to the waves created when a heavy object is thrown into a still pool of water. These sound waves, vibrations, or frequencies affect not only our physical form, but also our so-called subtle bodies—the emotional and mental field in which we live.

Our words are a major force in shaping our personal reality.

Through repetition of specific patterns we create laws for ourselves. The subconscious mind is influenced by our habitual trend of speaking. As a result, we are always making suggestions to ourselves, which tend to become self-fulfilling prophecies. By our speech we decree what will come into our life.

This helps to explain the rationale for the practice of "mantras" and "decrees"—word formulas that produce a heightened awareness and cause specific results. The sound itself, through its vibrational potency, brings about a change not only in the speaker, but also in the environment.

Your words create a web of subtle energy around you that gradually crystallizes into the actual disposition of your physical body. Negative speech over time creates a slumping, hunched posture. Vibrant, positive thoughts and words make the body upright and healthy. Habitual speech, as also habitual thought, affects your physical organs and your health. Profanity, slander, and foolish speech imprison one in a kind of vibratory web. In many cases, people prone to negative speaking habits create a "sound wall" between themselves and their higher consciousness. We improve our lives when we strive to utter only significant speech.

The law of the spoken word reaches its fulfillment in the practice of blessing. To bless means "to speak good"—to speak well of yourself and others. When you utter blessings, you activate beneficial forces through your speech.

A facet of the practice of blessing is the technique of affirmation. Affirmation is saying *yes* to life. It is a means of healing and renewal. When your words are positive and life-bestowing, you will create a more beautiful future for yourself and others. When we mentally affirm truth, we create a consciousness of success and capability. When we speak these affirmations aloud, we stir up forces on the physical plane which go forth like a swarm of invisible helpers, working to produce positive results.

The combination of affirmations with silent or spoken prayers is truly an awesome power. Many people have realized their goals and life ambitions by using prayer along with affirmations in a consistent and persistent manner. Jan Ross is a gifted and internationally-known intuitive who has helped and inspired thousands of people over her long career. She owns a popular bookstore in Phoenix, Arizona, which bears her name. She told me that she established and built her impressive store through the positive power of prayer and affirmations. Like Jan Ross, many successful people have used prayer, invocations, and spoken affirmations to help construct the life they desire.

For our words to regain their full magic, we must begin to master our thoughts and feelings. The origin of speech lies in our innermost thoughts, moods and reflections. Those who use the gift of speech to speak well of others are releasing constructive, healing forces into the world. All our words are seeds that eventually manifest their fruit.

Conversation is an area of immense potential for service and personal growth. A kind, helpful word is enough to change a person's mood, or alter their day's experience. Words can change a person's life. We have a great responsibility to use words carefully and constructively.

Conversation is an art. Few realize the power and potential of constructive conversation. Most people complain and criticize, find fault with others, or bemoan their lot in life. If we use speech and conversation consciously as a field of helpful expression, we find that we are presented with many moments through the course of a day in which to help others and make progress ourselves. It has been said that "Good words are worth much and cost little."

"There is always something beautiful to be found if we look for it," said White Eagle. A beautiful story from the early apocryphal writings illustrates this truth. The story describes Jesus walking with his disciples when they come upon a dead animal, half-rotted and partially eaten by scavengers. The disciples groan and exclaim at the stench and decay. After a moment of silence Jesus remarks to them, "What beautiful teeth the creature had!"

Truly, our words are magic powers which do much to determine our life. Once they pass our lips they are gone forever. There is a powerful example of the decisive nature of speech which comes from Shakespeare's drama of *King Lear*. The tragic king learns that his beloved daughter, Cordelia, has been sentenced to death. Lear sends a desperate command to halt the execution, but the message arrives too late. The previous order has been carried out and the devoted Cordelia is dead. Our words set in motion forces that sometimes cannot be retracted. The great Bulgarian philosopher, Mikhael Aivanhov, tells the following story of Mohammed to illustrate this truth.

One day a man came to Mohammed and voiced his sadness and frustration. He was miserable at himself for having argued angrily with a friend. He felt sorrow for his unkind words and asked the Prophet what he should do to make amends. Mohammed told the man to go around town placing feathers on the steps of many homes. He instructed the man to leave the feathers during the night and retrieve them in the morning, then he was to report back to Mohammed.

The next day the man returned with a look of distress on his face. "Mohammed," he cried. "I did as you told me, but when I returned this morning to gather the feathers, I could not find a single one!"

"So is it also with your words," explained the Prophet, "for they have flown from you and done their work, never to be recalled again."

If we find we have used ill-advised words or have spoken unkindly, the best remedy is to speak good words in their place. This may heal the damage we have caused. But as the above stories illustrate, it may never be possible to completely erase the ill effect of harmful speech. "Govern your tongue above all things," advised Pythagoras. Words are a major force in shaping our destiny. Whenever we speak, the inner words of our soul "become flesh and dwell among us."

Our words are also the medium by which agreements are made. This is the basis for a healthy society based on stability and truth. In ancient times, a person's word was their oath. It was a bond, an agreement, and was considered a sacred trust. So many problems today come about because people take their word lightly and lack sincerity when they speak. Many of today's social problems could be remedied with one simple solution. Keep all agreements. If people would honor their verbal and written agreements, a host of unnecessary government and legal functions would be eliminated. Keeping one's word is the foundation of a civilized society.

When we realize the extraordinary nature of speech, we can use it to our own and other people's advantage. The ancient practice of speaking to plants is rooted in this great power of sound to influence. By using affirmations, declarations and spoken prayers, we can help to bring harmony into our lives and our environment.

The nature of our words, the type of music to which we listen, and the general "audio environment" in which we live, have a tremendous influence in shaping who we are.

The science of the spoken word is still in its infancy. In the age to come, it will be a profound science, part of the new curriculum of the spiritual sciences.

*******

**Polishing the Jewel: Releasing the Magic of the Spoken Word**

Activity # one

Be conscious of your words and your conversations. If you find yourself speaking critically of someone, make a point to say something positive about them. Never end a conversation on a negative note. Find something constructive and helpful to say.

This is not to be mistaken for flattery, which implies saying something nice in order to obtain a favor. The objective here is to transform speech into a positive, life-bestowing tool. Remember that your tongue is a magic wand with tremendous power to shape your world.

Activity # two

Get into the habit of speaking positive affirmations aloud, provided that you are alone, of course. When in company, mentally affirm constructive thoughts and declarations. Send forth silent or spoken blessings to those who cross your path during the day. It is possible to stop a fight just by sending the combatants a stream of silent blessings.

<u>Activity # three</u>

Here's an old technique that can be as amusing as it is effective. Stand in front of a mirror and speak positively and lovingly to yourself as you look at your image. At first this might seem comical, or even slightly ridiculous. But it can be a great way to uplift your mood and energize your feelings. If for some reason you lack confidence on a particular day, give it a try. The worst that could happen is that you have a good laugh at your own expense.

## Affirmations

*"My words are a magic force with which I transform my life for the better."*

*"May the words of my lips heal, bless, uplift and encourage."*

*"May all those with whom I speak be helped by my words."*

# CHAPTER SIX
## The Sixth Jewel — The Magic of Gratitude

*"Persist in giving thanks*
*Even if you don't feel like it*
*and can see no earthly reason for it,*
*and the river of gladness and gratitude*
*will find its way into and through you."*
— Anonymous, *Turning*

*"Gratitude is the heart's memory."* — French proverb

*"The pearl is the oyster's autobiography."* — Federico Fellini

The key to a right orientation in life is found in the attitude of thankfulness. To be grateful is to have a divine perspective on events. The secret to a life of blessings—to a living philosophy of life—is to express gratitude for what life brings.

The journey each of us has traveled in life is a living book containing great wisdom. We discover the essence of that wisdom when we contemplate the events of our life with clarity and acceptance. Though we all have experiences we regret, we must forgive ourselves, admitting that at least we have been led by the events of life to this point of present understanding. We can be grateful, even joyous, for the flashes of insight and jewels of wisdom we have made our own.

Many people bemoan their fate and curse their conditions. The wise know that all events occur for a deeper reason—even if that reason remains a mystery. Difficulties, trials and hardship are often the sources of life's greatest transformations. Life's challenges create the very conditions that call forth our hidden splendor, the spark of greatness that often lies dormant within us. Within each difficulty lies a seed of a greater good. A grateful attitude enables us to look for and discover the gems that lie buried beneath the turmoil of life. Often, acceptance and gratitude for a small good will open the way for a still greater benefit to come into our life.

There is something of value hidden within every difficult experience. When we can accept with gratitude even the harsh experiences in life and train ourselves to look for the potential good that comes to us from these experiences, we extract a mysterious essence which transforms us. Our disappointments often teach us our most valuable lessons.

This compensatory feature in life offers us a jewel beneath the jagged surface of difficulties—sweet fruit beyond the thorns. The highest attitude is to be grateful for everything—to see everything as a blessing, a stepping stone to greater self-knowledge and ultimately to better circumstances.

Because of the conditions of physical life, it is natural to go through periods of sorrow and suffering. Even Jesus and Buddha wept on occasion. Sadness and trials are teachers on the path of inner unfolding. All the harsh experiences of life come in order to break the shell of selfishness and open the heart to the realities of a larger universe. "The deeper that sorrow carves into your heart," said Kahlil Gibran, "the more joy you can contain." We can lessen our suffering if we seek to discover the pearl within the painful conditions of life. By reflecting without resentment on experience, searching for the jewels of wisdom, we elevate our consciousness. This releases us from suffering. If we can accept that all events tend ultimately towards good for all involved, we will experience an inner awakening and a gradual understanding of the universal laws that govern life.

Challenges bring with them the opportunity for growth. It is the pressure that creates a diamond. The irritant within the oyster creates the pearl. Even in climbing a mountain, we depend on rough spots and irregularities to provide foot and handholds. It has been said that one of the traits of the enlightened mind is that it sees the good element in even the darkest of experiences. It is certainly true that if we look for the potential benefit in our disappointments, we can transform those experiences, taking some if not all of the sting out.

When I was teaching a class of fifth graders in California, we were practicing penmanship with refillable fountain pens. On every desk was a little jar of black or blue ink. The students were illustrating their history lesson books with pictures about the events. A girl named Nawana had just finished drawing a beautiful crayon illustration of a wooden ship on the sea. As she proudly showed me her work, the student in front leaned back and tipped over Nawana's black ink jar, blotting the entire page. Nawana burst into tears. I sponged up the ink and held up the notebook to dry, then set it back on Nawana's desk. The ink had not affected the wax crayon image and the colors remained vivid. Only the white portion of the paper had turned an inky black. "It's a night scene!" Nawana exclaimed with enthusiasm. Sure enough, the illustration had lost none of its beauty and in some ways was even more interesting as a "night scene." Both Nawana and I had learned a lesson in turning "negatives to positives."

Many people owe their achievements to the tremendous challenges they faced. Wolfgang Amadeus Mozart, the most beloved of all composers, produced his most extraordinary musical works in a period of acute outer grief and misery. Despite his suffering, he infused a quality of joy into his compositions that has never been surpassed. It is as if his spirit sought to transcend the misery of his circumstances by drawing upon a fountain of inspiration that lay forever beyond the reach of mortal sorrow. As a result, there is something immortal in Mozart's music.

Thankfulness is an attitude which can be cultivated—cherished—so that it develops into a feature of character. This enables one to transform obstacles into stepping stones. Ordeals become the experiences that lead to enlightenment. Fear, negation and a gloomy frame of mind cannot exist in a mental atmosphere of thanksgiving.

Gratitude releases a light in our minds which chases the darkness. Like an inner sun, its bright beams dry up the gloomy swamps of anxiety and depression. Its presence within our consciousness stirs and awakens forces that lead to constructive actions and courageous efforts. We ignite the spark of happiness in our hearts when we express an inner attitude of thanksgiving. Constant gratitude fans this tiny spark into a flame of joy.

The thankful attitude may be compared to an elixir drawn from the deep reservoir of the soul. Like a divine tonic, it produces contentment and a sense of well-being. Thankfulness is a healing balm that dissolves the toxins produced by a bitter and resentful state of mind. Gratitude grants strength and enthusiasm for living.

Thankfulness is one of the soul's most beautiful qualities. People who express gratitude emanate an intangible quality of magnanimity—literally, "greatness of soul." Gratitude expands the radiance of the heart and triggers a response from the larger life of which we are a part. The grateful state of mind puts one in touch with a universe of immeasurable power.

An important characteristic of gratitude is that it not only enhances the quality of life, but it increases our ability to achieve our goals and expand our prosperity. When we express gratitude for the good we have, we open up hidden channels of supply. We prepare the way for the reception of even greater good. Gratitude has an almost magical power to create opportunities and release the flow of abundance.

In the estimate of many, money is the most desirable com- modity on earth. We all know that money is essential in modern life, but there is so much that is of far greater value. How much money would you give in trade for your eyes? Would you part with your thumb for a million dollars? Is any tangible value of equal worth to the happiness that comes through the birth of a child? Can you put a price tag on the natural wonders of the world? It is precisely through our earthly experiences that we extract a quintessence, an extract bought at the price of our struggles, mistakes, triumphs and tragedies. Is it possible to place an economic value on the wisdom we gain from our life experi- ence?

It is well to remember that the universe in which we live has bestowed upon us many extraordinary gifts. The stars, the seas, the forests, and the natural wonders of the world are an awe- inspiring treasury—an infinite storehouse—of magnificence and mystery. So much comes to us each day that is the result of the labors of others—most of whom we do not know. All of this is cause for profound gratitude.

The grateful state of mind releases a force from within yourself which, like a breath of the divine, will work to eliminate negativity from your life. Gratitude brings inner peace, serenity and tranquillity of spirit—the precursors of true wisdom. Gratitude counters arrogance and false pride, negative qualities which turn people away.

Gratitude is an inexhaustible source of renewal, growth and rejuvenation. When we express thankfulness by our inner attitude, we release a mysterious power from our minds and hearts that has a healing, beneficial influence. We begin to emanate an indefinable quality that others feel or perceive and which attracts them to us.

Gratitude smoothes out countless difficulties and unlocks a portal into nature's treasurehouse of safeguarded secrets—a portal which remains forever sealed to the ungrateful. Those who give thanks for life's blessings come under the influence of higher beings. If we live in accordance with the laws which govern life, living becomes an ever-unfolding miracle.

Gratitude is the magic that leads to a happy life.

\*\*\*\*\*\*\*\*

## Polishing the Jewel: Releasing the Magic of Gratitude

### Activity # one

Think of someone who has done you a favor or helped you in some way for which you never expressed gratitude. Perhaps a friend or relative will come to mind, possibly one or both of your parents. Write that person or those persons a card or letter thanking them for their help or inspiration. Or, if you prefer, pick up the telephone and call them.

<u>Activity # two</u>

Make a list of all the benefits and blessing of your life. Reflect deeply on all of the good things that have come your way and all the beautiful experiences you have had. Practice saying "thank you" mentally as often as you can during the day. It has been said that the highest prayer, the most effective mantra, is composed of the two simple words: "thank you."

## Affirmations

*"I give thanks this day for my wonderful life and the opportunities for growth and happiness."*

*I live forever in a beautiful, marvelous creation. I give thanks to the countless beings who have made my existence possible."*

*"I know that as I create an attitude of thanksgiving in my mind, I increase my ability to draw all good into my life."*

*"All things are working together for good in my life."*

# CHAPTER SEVEN
## The Seventh Jewel — The Magic of Manifesting

*"We must attune and harmonize ourselves with Cosmic Intelligence by vibrating on the same wavelength and creating true beauty."* — O. Mikhael Aivanhov

Every human being is naturally creative. We are constantly creating each moment of our lives—by virtue of our thoughts and feelings, as well as by our actions. It is true that the creations of most people do not amount to very much, for they have never tapped the inexhaustible powers at their disposal. And in some cases this is good, for numerous people might only stir up mischief—even chaos—if they truly understood the secret of their power.

But the truth is that we are creative spirits by nature. Not only do we have the power to fashion our lives, but the circumstances in which we currently find ourselves have been created by the thoughts and emotions we have previously entertained, albeit often unconsciously.

It has been said that "the entire universe rearranges itself to fit your picture of reality." This has a nice ring to it, but is not completely true. Our opinion of the law of gravity, for instance, does not change the operation of this law. We may think that the sun moves around the earth, but our misperception will not influence these heavenly bodies.

The fact is that the larger universe in which we find ourselves—the *macrocosm*, or "greater whole"—is the creation of higher beings. Our personal opinions—our "picture of reality"—will not alter the universal laws. What *is* true is that we fashion our *personal universe* in the image of our own minds and hearts. It is a truth of great significance that we are the shapers of our individual destiny. Thus it is accurate to say that our personal world rearranges itself to fit our picture of reality.

In the ancient world, the deeper truths of life were taught in the "Mystery Schools" or temples. Eleusis, a small town just outside of Athens, was a principal center of culture in the Mediterranean for nearly 1000 years. In the temples of Eleusis, sacred dramas were enacted to illustrate the laws of life. Candidates for initiation were shown a vision of Hades, or the "underworld." This was a ghastly place, where unfortunate souls were tormented by a host of frightening creatures and circumstances. Following this scene, the participants in the Mysteries were shown a vision of the Elysian Fields, a heavenly state of splendor, beauty, and ceaseless happiness.

The initiates were made to understand that they created their own future conditions, both on earth and in the afterlife, by the quality of their thoughts, feelings and actions. Destructive thoughts, words, emotions, and deeds would lead to conditions represented by the vision of Hades. Conversely, luminous thinking and activities would lead to circumstances represented by the grandeur of Elysium. The participants current environment and position in life was not the result of an arbitrary decision made by a whimsical deity, nor was it due to "chance." The conditions in

which all individuals found themselves was the result of processes they themselves had previously set in motion, either in this life
or an earlier one. According to the luminous wisdom of the
ancient Mysteries, each man and woman holds the key to the
future in their own hands.

Your current circumstances did not happen by accident. You
caused them by the manner in which you have concentrated all
the years of your existence. The formative principle that shapes
substance is mind. When you focus your mind on a visual scenario, you are forcing into your field of experience the very
scenes you visualize. What the mind conceives, it eventually
receives, so long as the intention is strong enough.

The part feeling and desire play in this process of creation or
manifestation cannot be too greatly emphasized. Desire is emotion that is filled with the yearnings of the heart. The more powerful the feeling within a desire, the more rapidly it tends to be
realized. It is advisable to guard our feelings and desires, for they
are the gateways to experience. Emotion is a mighty force—life's
dynamic principle—which always leads to action. Feelings and
desires are the bridge by which thoughts become physical realities.

You've probably guessed that the law of manifestation is the
synthesis of all the "jewels" presented so far. The fruits of the law
of the seed, the collective impact of our thoughts, emotion,
actions, and speech—along with an attitude of thankfulness—are
the magic forces by which we fashion our lives and our circumstances. When we use all these together, not only do we consciously create our future, but we can begin to predict it.

In ancient Greece, the Oracle of Delphi was famed for its
accuracy in forecasting the future. The priestess in the temple of

Apollo was admired throughout the world for her pithy utterances of events to come. In fact, the word *pithy* comes from the Delphic Oracle. The temple priestesses were known as "pythonesses"—or *pythia*—and this term became synonymous with a brief, astute remark. We can work our own oracle in daily life when we use the powers of mind, emotion, imagination, and will in a consistent effort to achieve our goals. Results are certain to follow if we work with determination and persistence.

There is an additional means by which we can harness all these forces for maximum benefit. This is the power of concentration. Concentration is the focusing of mental attention on a specific topic. It may be compared to the power of a magnifying glass to focus the rays of the sun. Just as a magnifying glass can burn a hole through wood or ignite a flame, so can the focused mind penetrate to the solution of a problem, or spark new ideas and insights.

The laser is an even better example of concentration. A laser amplifies light into a single beam of incredible power. Essentially, a laser is a ruby rod surrounded by a spiral lamp. When the lamp is on, the chromium atoms of the ruby are stimulated. When the stimulation is sufficiently great, a narrow beam of light extends from the ruby crystal. This is the laser beam, which because of its intensity and consistent wave vibration, has unusual power.

The spiral lamp, which stimulates or "excites" the chromium atoms in the ruby rod, may be compared to our emotions. When we are sufficiently interested in something, our enthusiasm stimulates the "molecules of our mind," represented by the ruby rod. By focusing the light of our intentions and our dreams through mental concentration, we can achieve remarkable results very rapidly.

Not only is concentration induced more easily when we feel enthused about something, but the act of mental focusing will itself awaken interest and enthusiasm in any area of study. A teacher of mine in junior high once told me that a person who learns to concentrate will never be bored again.

The power of concentration is a magical tool that can create or destroy, depending upon the subject of our attention and the nature of our thoughts. Hence the saying of the Buddha: "Suffering follows an evil thought as the wheels of a cart follow the oxen that draw it. Joy follows a good thought like a shadow that never leaves." Constructive thoughts build a bridge to a better life. Destructive thoughts harden into chains that enslave us. When we refrain from discordant thinking, our circumstances improve. For every mental cause there follows a physical result. Positive thoughts will produce like effects.

One of the most remarkable individuals I've ever had the privilege to meet is the American spiritual teacher, Peter Rosen. Seeing him for the first time was a truly memorable moment in my life. I realized I was standing face-to-face with an enlightened man—someone who lives and breathes the deeper truths of life. Peter exemplifies in his life an extraordinary knowledge and mastery of the laws of manifestation. In the wonderful little book entitled, *The Magic Man*, by "Friends of Peter," a number of people whose lives he has touched have compiled some notable examples of his creative and enlightened approach to life.

Peter has a remarkable relationship to animals. There are usually a number of wild bears sleeping on the deck of his delightful home, which he built with his friends on a picturesque site overlooking the Smoky Mountains above Gatlinburg, Tennessee. Once, while walking in the woods near his home, he encountered a female bear that was soon to give birth. Peter spoke gently to the bear and lay down in the forest, letting her sniff his face and beard. Weeks later the mother bear came bounding to Peter's house with the little cub trailing behind.

There have been many seemingly "miraculous" healings around him. Once he lay his hands on a young boy's broken foot. Minutes later the boy stood up and walked without his crutches. He loves to play little "tricks" and games, like pouring wine from his finger or making it snow. But the greatest manifestations are the changes wrought in people's lives by Peter's loving and enlightened example. As he would be the first to say, all of us have in ourselves the extraordinary power of our deeper self, waiting to blossom into full creative expression. Individuals like Peter Rosen remind us of the awesome creative might within each of us.

I once heard a teacher describing the law of manifestation— that we each create our personal reality—to some newcomers to that notion. This teacher said that if the idea made them uncomfortable, possibly because they felt guilty for the mess they'd made of things so far, they should forget the idea—as if they'd never heard of it—and go back to living as if things just happened by chance.

This approach is like a person who, upon learning about the law of gravity says, "that makes me uncomfortable; I don't know if I can accept it," and is then advised by a physicist to go on living as if there were no such thing as gravity and they had never heard about it.

This is an unrealistic position—an expression of denial. We are here to learn these eternal truths and apply them to our lives. The result will be self-mastery. Nothing matters essentially except our ability to control our own lives. We may have an encyclopedic knowledge, but if we do not have the power to transform our circumstances and our environment, we have simply missed the point.

Many people entering upon a spiritual path have a tendency to become dependent on someone they regard as their "guru" or "master"—often surrendering even basic life decisions to that person. They risk giving away their own power of spiritual discernment and personal authority, thus setting back their spiritual development. Peter Rosen suggests the following for people inclined to look outside themselves for authority figures. Stand in front of the mirror each morning and say, "I'm responsible for my life; what am I going to do about it?" That is a healthy approach.

As stated previously, all things in the physical world have been created from mind. Our thoughts, feelings, desires—and the decisions and choices we make as a result of them—are the building blocks of life. For each mental cause there is a physical consequence. When you fashion an idea, it gives birth to a form. Because all physical creations or manifestations are the results of thoughts, it follows that by working with these ideas we can create the kind of life we want. Even our facial features and bodily characteristics reflect the influence of our habitual thought and feeling. A story from Abraham Lincoln's life illustrates this truth.

As President, Lincoln often met with private citizens. For several days a man kept trying to see him, but each time he would attempt to make an appointment, the President declined. One of his aides asked why he adamantly refused to meet the visitor. Lincoln replied that he could tell by the man's face that he had nothing constructive to say and that meeting with him would only be a waste of time. The aide expressed dismay that Lincoln would judge the man on the basis of his external features. Lincoln replied that it would indeed be wrong to judge a young person on facial characteristics, but that after age forty, a person's face begins to take on the cast of his or her dominant thoughts and emotions. Lincoln himself is an example of this truth.

Lincoln's face was not beautiful by any conventional standard. It was plain and homely. Yet upon his features were sculpted the qualities of patience, compassion, sacrifice, and deep spiritual insight. The change in his features between the year of his first inauguration and the time of his tragic death are a testimony to those four years of anguish. This great soul mirrored the suffering and trials of a nation during its severest spiritual crisis. Lincoln's immortal spirit etched its genius and love into his rough countenance and as a result will always have the power to awaken admiration in the hearts and minds of those who contemplate his features. Few individuals have been as universally loved as Abraham Lincoln.

Thought waves gradually densify or crystallize into the "stuff" we call matter. This holds true also for our physical bodies. We create our bodies according to our mental images. The frequencies of thought create the geometry of the body. In other words, the soul is the template of the body—or more accurately—the soul creates a multi-dimensional template through which our three-dimensional physical body crystallizes. We are liquid light poured into a geometric chrysalis.

The metaphysical basis for the law of manifestation is the law of affinity, or the fact that "like attracts like." This principle of affinity is called in physics the law of acoustic resonance. This law is known to all musicians. If you pluck the string of a violin, the same string of a second, identically-tuned violin will begin to vibrate in sympathetic attunement. The same experiment can be done with tuning forks of the same pitch. In like manner, our inner life of moods and feelings, ideas and sentiments, stirs up a response or *resonance* from the universal life in which we are imbedded.

In the ancient Mystery Schools, this truth was expressed in the *Hermetic Axiom*, usually translated as, "That which is below is as that which is above, and that which is without is as that which is within, for the working of the one law." In plain English, this means that your inner world of thought and feeling creates your outer world of circumstance. As a result of this law, we magnetize to ourselves people, circumstances and conditions that correspond in nature to what we emanate from our inner life of thoughts, feelings and attitudes. Thus our inner world is the prototype of our outer world.

The law of affinity is a more subtle explanation of the law of the seed. On the finer levels of energy and vibration, our emanations at any given moment set up an immediate response from the universal life in which we find ourselves. Thus we can perceive a most remarkable characteristic of the law of the seed. The consequences we experience as a result of our actions occur in a two-fold manner. In the world of thought or consciousness there is an instantaneous effect. On the "physical plane," which is governed by the experience of time, there is a secondary effect that will bear fruit in the future.

Perhaps the best way to understand this is through the analogy of planting actual seeds in a literal garden. You know that the seeds you plant, say pumpkin seeds, will only bear fruit after several months. But the activity of planting gives you immediate experiences as well. These are the bodily and emotional sensations that accompany the gardening activity—the benefits of exercise and fresh air, for instance. The same is true for all actions, even the most subtle activities of consciousness. Every thought and feeling that we experience sets up an immediate response from the cosmos that will be an exact reflection of the nature of our thoughts, feelings, and actions. In this way the universe at all moments reflects back to us—mirror-like—exactly who we are. In addition, we will experience an effect later in time that is also the fruit of our deeds.

The immediate response from the universal "ocean of existence" elicited by the law of affinity helps explain the mysterious "coincidences" and synchronicities that occur in life. The inner connection between external events and what goes on in our minds may be linked in this way and may have more of a causal basis than many psychologists believe. The law of affinity also helps us understand the wonderful, serendipitous feeling of being "in the flow" of life. This marvelous state of attunement is a result of an inner harmony that links us to the deep underlying harmony of the universe.

By comprehending this truth we can begin to shape our life as we wish by becoming conscious of what goes on in our minds. Becoming aware of our thoughts is the first step, but we must not stop here. To achieve really significant results, we need to take charge of our minds and focus selectively on what we choose. Thoughts, feelings, and desires are the stallions that lead your chariot through life. You are the charioteer who must guide and direct these powerful forces so that they take you where you want to go. We create better external conditions when we improve the quality of our habitual states of feeling and mind.

This idea of affinity is closely related to the notion that those with whom we associate have tremendous influence upon us. An ancient spiritual maxim holds that those who would develop inwardly and advance towards enlightenment should be very careful with whom they habitually associate. The type of "crowd" one draws into one's sphere of activity will have great impact on the direction one takes in life. The cliché is true that "birds of a feather flock together." Change your "feathers"—that is, your thoughts, feelings, interests and habitual moods—and you will attract a different kind of "bird."

Each of us is wrapped in an energy envelope, or aura, composed of our psychic and thought emanations. Our aura may be a nasty collection of colors, particles and residues, or a place of beauty and light. Our auric field may act as a protective shield or as a festering swamp that attracts all manner of undesirable creatures. It depends on the materials—our thoughts and feelings—that go to create it.

Although our inner life of mind, heart and soul is responsible for the external world we inhabit, it is well to recognize that the ultimate creation of each soul is the soul itself. John Keats, the great English romantic poet, said that we are on earth to forge our souls. Like a spider weaving its web, we spin the strands of our inner life, creating a shining tapestry or a dark web that entraps us. We choose the elements that go to form our inner world, and in so doing we fashion who we are.

If you desire to improve your disposition, begin now to introduce more optimistic thoughts into your consciousness. You may even find yourself invited to the heavenly banquets—the communion of the angels and saintly masters. At least we can prepare to become worthy. Ultimately, our disposition will be our calling card. The lines of Henley are eternally true: "I am the master of my fate, I am the captain of my soul."

*******

**Polishing the Jewel: Releasing the Magic of Manifesting**

Think of something you want or desire. It could be an intangible quality or a virtue, but for this exercise a material object is best. It should be a "stretch," that is, something requiring effort,—perhaps a new computer, a car, a bicycle, a fine piece of jewelry, or a new living situation. It could be a gift you want to give someone. Give yourself from 2-4 weeks in which to obtain the item. Write down what you want. Visualize it clearly, in minute detail. Then devise a plan for acquiring it. Think about your objective every day.

Remarkable events often happen with conscious manifesting. Sometimes the item you seek will be given to you. It's perfectly all right just to go out and purchase it. But it should be something requiring effort, not something you ordinarily might buy. Unless it is a major acquisition, try not going into debt. If you use "credit," be sure you are in a position to make timely payments so as not to hurt yourself financially.

The purpose of this exercise is to gain confidence in the laws which underlie the process. We draw to ourselves that upon which we focus our attention and for which we exert effort. Of course, material gains are of far less importance than the ability to change character and acquire new habits of thought and feeling. The ultimate "manifestations" are developing the virtues of a more enlightened consciousness. Use this exercise as a stepping stone to the acquisition of qualities of enduring value—determination, the light of understanding, and a loving heart.

## Affirmations

*"I am the source of my experience. I am the author of my life. I am creating a more beautiful future for myself by improving the quality of my inner world."*

*"All that I need and more is coming my way. I live in a world of abundance and beauty."*

*"I am transforming myself into a being of light, love, wisdom and ability."*

# CHAPTER EIGHT
## The Eighth Jewel — The Magic of Faith

*"The dice of God are always loaded."* — Emerson

*"Trust in God, but tie up your camel."* — Unknown

Little is possible in life without faith. The inner attitude we call belief, or faith, is a tremendous power. Faith does not mean a blind belief in a dogmatic position of a scientific or ecclesiastical authority. It is a conviction that comes with life experience and spiritual maturity—as one begins to make contact with the radiant inner source of wisdom and power.

Though faith has always been associated with religion, and many great saints have developed a high degree of this quality, essentially it has nothing to do with external doctrines. Faith means an unwavering assurance in the infallibility of divine laws. It is a deep certainty, an unswerving conviction, that the laws and principles that govern life always work.

These laws of life—the cornerstones of the universe—are active always and everywhere. When we act, we may rest assured that the universe will react. The universal laws will bring justice. These laws are not human inventions. They operate with or without human belief, just as gravity is in operation whether you believe in it or not.

In this sense these laws are entirely impersonal; they aren't swayed by personality or by externals. Money, power, and prestige cannot corrupt them. For this reason, Justice is depicted with a blindfold. She looks not at outer appearance, but at the motives of the heart. She is not swayed by social position or worldly eminence, but looks objectively at our actions.

External social codes and customs change often, and nowadays most societies are not based upon a perception of these higher truths. But the eternal laws devised by universal intelligence are unchanging. Human beings may discover these laws, but cannot alter them.

Those who doubt that absolute law governs life become unsure of themselves. To those as yet unschooled in the eternal wisdom, life seems uncertain, arbitrary, even whimsical. Faith is the opposite of doubt and uncertainty. It is a deep-seated conviction that the laws governing life are good, wise, just and true—and that these divine principles operate in all circumstances.

Certain remarkable people have developed this faculty to an unusual degree, causing seeming miracles to occur around them and in their lives. Faith, or belief, becomes a power that triggers a response from the hidden dimensions of life—a response that can at times seem almost magical or supernatural. The lives of saints and deeply religious people are full of such incidents. A wonderful example comes from the life of St. Francis.

In his travels through the Italian countryside, Francis lingered some days in a forest with the loyal brother monks who later became the nucleus of the Franciscan order. Word of St. Francis' whereabouts spread among the nearby villages, and people journeyed by the hundreds to catch a glimpse of the beloved saint. More arrived by the hour and the gathering soon swelled to a large crowd.

The brothers became nervous, for they had no food of their own and the people had brought little with them. It grew late in the day and the brothers feared that the people, many of whom were ill and elderly, would begin to suffer.

Again and again Francis told them that all would be well—that they would be amply cared for by Providence. The brothers remained unconvinced. Then in the late afternoon, several wagonloads arrived, heavily laden with food, blankets and provisions. A wealthy merchant had heard of the gathering and wanted to send a gift to Francis and the people. As they passed out the food and provisions, the brothers rejoiced at the "miracle," and marveled at the faith of their leader.

Events like these—which might be termed "miracles of faith"—are still within the province of universal law. It in no way demeans the greatness of St. Francis if we see a miracle like this in the light of the law of affinity. Francis was able to set in motion certain currents by the qualities of his inner life which produced a response—a sympathetic resonance—from the "universal mind," or from the spiritual beings who act as the agents of these universal principles. The law of affinity draws to us what is in accordance with the conditions of our inner world.

Walter Russell, who I will speak of again in the next chapter, displayed a great faith in the unseen universal power. An extraordinary incident in his youth demonstrates this faith. In 1886, as a boy of fifteen working himself through art school, he promised his girlfriend he would take her to a whole series of operas that cost almost eighty dollars—more money than he had ever held in his hand. The day the box office opened, he stood in line to get tickets behind a long row of people. Despite having only six dollars in his pocket, he believed absolutely in his heart that by the time he reached the window he would have the full amount. Then a stranger approached him with a request that Walter Russell recognized as an opportunity. In his marvelous little book entitled *The Man Who Tapped the Secrets of the Universe*, Glenn Clark describes the incident as follows:

> In the morning a man said to him, "Sonny, would you like to make $5.00?"
> "Yes, sir, how?"
> "By selling me your place in line so I can get to my office by nine."
> Quick as a flash he replied. "I'll do better for you than that. Give me the money and I will deliver the tickets to you." Without even asking his name, the man gave him the money and his address, and he put it down in a notebook. Holding the money between his fingers and with notebook and pencil in hand, looking like a bookmaker at the races, he became a magnet drawing scores of people to him. By the time he reached the box office he had the amount necessary for the entire series...and $110.00 in excess, enough to carry him through months of school. The strange thing was that no one even asked him his name and address!

This remarkable anecdote shows that seeming miracles are truly possible when one trusts wholeheartedly in the universal powers.

If we act with faith and conviction, little "miracles" of serendipity will often come about. When Mia and I returned from Mexico one summer, we spent the last of our money buying gifts, saving only enough for the hotel in San Francisco the night of our return. But we forgot about the Mexican airport tax. After paying the tax, we arrived in San Francisco at midnight with no checks or credit cards and only enough cash for transportation to the hotel. We calmly told ourselves that we had done all we could and that we could trust in the universal supply of abundance to come to our aid.

When the taxi arrived at the hotel, we paid the driver ten dollars, literally the last of our money, and calmly stepped out into the street. There on the sidewalk was a five dollar bill, which Mia deftly scooped up. We persuaded the hotel to take that as a deposit on the room until we could go to the bank the next day, smiling to each other at our little "miracle."

Years earlier, when I was a youthful student in England, I had an unexpected and somewhat grueling test of my patience and my faith. Some friends and I decided to escape the winter by going to the beaches of North Africa during Christmas break. Hoping to save money—a student's most precious commodity— we decided to camp out on the beach in sleeping bags. At the last minute my friends backed out, but I was undeterred. Always in the mood for an adventure, I continued on alone. I journeyed by train through Europe, then flew from Rome to Tunis, site of the ancient city of Carthage and home of the legendary conqueror, Hannibal the Great.

All went well for a few sunny days, but then one morning I rather stupidly left my backpack and sleeping bag in a lemon grove and returned to find them gone. This was before the day of universal credit cards, and I was forced to spend my limited money in hotels. Cutting short my holiday, I decided to return to England. Even then, I was so short on funds that I had to sell my coat to a merchant to scrape up a bit more cash. I had my plane ticket to Palermo, Sicily and enough money to buy a train ticket from there to the French Riviera. That was it.

I arrived in Palermo in the evening and bought my train ticket, but the train left the next day and I hadn't money for even the cheapest hotel. So I walked for several hours in downtown Palermo, wondering what to do. Years later I would live in Rome, but at the time I couldn't speak a word of Italian. I had thought I might sleep in a park, but all the parks were fenced in and the gates were locked at night. Finally, at midnight, I paused on a downtown thoroughfare and leaned against a tree, exhausted and out of ideas. Glancing up, I realized what to do. Making sure no one was watching, I climbed the tree and cradled myself in its branches. Ever since that memorable night I've had a very high opinion of trees!

The train ride through Sicily and Italy was picturesque but interminably slow. Spending the last of my money on stale croissants, I finally arrived in Monte Carlo two days later, literally penniless. Figuring to hitch through France to the port of Calais and then by ferry on to Dover, I stood for two days in Monte Carlo without getting a ride. (With its fabulous beaches and famous gambling casinos, I began to see why Monte Carlo was known as a sunny place with a lot of shady characters!) At night I slept in a park. In desperation, I remembered I had the name of a friend of a friend—Nicole—who lived down the road from Monte Carlo. I called her and she came to meet me. She gave me the address of an American acquaintance in Paris, then bought me a train ticket to Lyons, France. I was speechless with gratitude.

Lyons was still a long way from Paris and the weather had turned bitterly cold. There was nothing to do but stick out my thumb again and hope for the best. As I stood by the freeway, shivering without my jacket, it began to snow. Fortunately, this time it was only a few hours before I got a ride to Paris with a jovial German businessman. I looked up my "friend's friend's acquaintance," a man named Patrick, and he let me stay at his place. On top of it all, he gave me a royal tour of Paris. Then he gave me about fifty dollars, enough money for a bus ticket to Calais and a ferry ride to Dover. I shall be forever grateful to him.(Though I later sent money to repay both Patrick and Nicole, they each were insistent that I not feel obligated by their help-fulness.) I arrived in Dover relieved, but once more penniless. A Belgian businessman gave me a ride to Sussex and I was soon back at my school in the cozy town of Forest Row, a little worn, but wiser by far. In addition to learning about the value of making contingency plans, I learned a bundle about the importance of faith and patience, and volumes about gratitude. Adversity teach-es us what nothing else can.

It would be a mistake to think that possessing faith means we should wait passively for some external power or a force outside ourselves to come to our aid. No doubt, there are many instances of miraculous intervention from the unseen dimensions, and of assistance from angels and spirit helpers. But the healthy cultiva-tion of faith relies on developing the attitude of mind that pro-pels us as individuals to do everything within our power to achieve our goals. We must do all we can, knowing that when we do, the universe will come to our aid. Each of us possesses the power to achieve what we seek. We release this seemingly "miraculous" power by consistent, positive efforts, coupled with an inner certainty that the laws of life always work.

From the Brothers Grimm comes a simple story illustrating

the transforming power of faith and a giving heart. A young orphan girl with nothing but a crust of bread and the clothes she is wearing, sets forth into the open country, "trusting in the good God." When she meets a poor man who asks her for some bread, she hands him the whole piece. Further along she comes upon a child who begs for some clothing to keep her warm. The good-hearted little girl gives the child her hood. Still further on she finds two more shivering children. To the first she gives her jacket and to the second she gives her frock. At last as evening falls she enters a forest. There she comes upon yet another child who begs the girl for her shirt. As it was fast becoming dark, and thinking that no one could see her, she gave away the very last of her possessions. As she stood there, alone and bereft, "suddenly some stars from heaven fell down." When she picked them up she saw that they had become shining pieces of gold. And though she had given away her shirt, yet another one appeared, made of the finest linen. The story concludes with the words, "And she was rich all the days of her life." This charming tale reminds us that when we give fully of ourselves, trusting in the beneficent laws, we elicit a response from the universal life of which we are a part.

Faith means acting with assurance, even before the outcome is known. Peter Rosen and his partner, Ann, demonstrated a remarkable degree of faith and vision when they moved from Fort Lauderdale to Gatlinburg, Tennessee. Peter told his friends that there was a thirteen acre parcel adjoining the National Forest that they would be able to buy. However, the Realtors assured them that no such parcel existed. (Gatlinburg is a resort town and developers would have long ago snatched up such an available piece of land.) Peter insisted that the land was there and they would be able to build their home and teaching center on it. So he, Ann, and a few close friends packed up their belongings and made the long move.

Three months cooped up in a rental home with near-constant rain was trying for virtually everyone—everyone except Peter. He was always happy and brimming with optimism. Sure enough, at the end of three months the "non-existent" parcel was "found"— bordered on three sides by the National Forest. At the same time the rain stopped, and they began to build the center known today as Mystic Mountain.

When Mia and I made the decision to leave California, we figured it would not be easy. We would have to sell two stores— each with less than two years remaining on the lease—as well as our home. We made a trip to Arizona to see if we liked it. We did, and decided to act boldly and swiftly. As we drove out of the charming town of Prescott three days later, we placed nonrefundable deposits to purchase a store that was going out of business, and a beautiful home nearby that we had driven up to "by accident." Having made an absolutely firm commitment to our goals, we acted instantly with a degree of confidence and "audacity" that almost surprised us.

That night we wrote down very specific affirmations to fit our goals of selling our home and two stores in California smoothly and easily, "under grace and in perfect ways." We prayed and affirmed our intentions both together and individually almost constantly during the next three months. Within a week of our return to California we had placed our home on the market. But we knew nothing about selling our businesses. We made some calls and were fortunate to find an attorney whose "hobby" was helping people sell their businesses. With his assistance, we put our two stores up for sale. At the same time, we did everything we could think of to make our home attractive, including painting it inside and out. On Easter Sunday, five weeks after we put the house on the market, we received our first offer on our home. A week later we received our first phone call about the business. Before eight weeks had passed, the sale of our home and both businesses had gone into escrow. Less than four months after making the decision to move, we had completed the deals on our home and businesses and were living in Arizona.

One of the extraordinary features of faith is that it constantly grows stronger when exercised. The faculty by which faith grows and becomes a dynamic power is the subconscious mind, what the Huna shamans of Hawaii call *ku*. The subconscious is a tremendous ally in our growth toward spiritual maturity and enlightenment. To free our consciousness from the oppressive memory of past error, we need to enlist the support of the subconscious dimensions of the mind and the emotions. We influence the subconscious by repetition of positive acts and thoughts, and by developing a conviction of the sure outworking of universal laws. The more powerful our feelings, the greater our capacity to activate the support of the subconscious.

The subconscious mind has awesome power and an extraordinary intelligence, far exceeding that of the conscious mind. Consider that it is the subconscious power of the body-mind that oversees all the complex functions of digestion, assimilation, metabolism, growth, all the organ functions, the operation of the endocrine system, reproduction, circulation, breathing and heartbeat. It is the subconscious wisdom operating through body that enables the physical organism to heal itself of injuries.

The conscious mind has virtually no knowledge of how this

incredibly complex system works. If it did understand and tried to interfere, it would probably only botch up the smooth inter-working of all these processes. It is not surprising that traditional metaphysics teaches that what we call the subconscious mind includes superconscious influences that are the work of higher beings—known for millennia as the divine hierarchies of angels—which include archangels, cherubim and seraphim.

We do know that one aspect of the subconscious mind is to work as a recording device and that it records all messages from the conscious mind and will act on these "orders." When we feed good, constructive suggestions to the subconscious, we gain the assistance of a prodigious ally. This aspect of the subconscious is like a mighty giant that is entirely obedient to our conscious com-mand. But this awesome giant needs to be convinced that we are a worthy master. It does not like taking orders from a proven weakling! We must show it that we are capable of worthy deeds and that we are able to establish authority within our life and within our physical organism. This means at least a measure of self-control.

The subconscious may be compared to the basement of a huge castle. It contains all the records and treasures of all our experiences. When we organize our subconscious through feeding it positive commands and affirmations, and when we put our house in order by constructive actions, we begin to harness this awesome power to be used for our benefit. We can begin to unlock this power by cleaning out our closets, figuratively and lit-erally, and getting our environment in shape. The subconscious does not like chaos. When we establish our life on constructive lines, the positive suggestions we give our subconscious will start to take effect. Though this work takes time, it is not difficult. It is delightful and satisfying to see the steady improvements which gradually unfold in one's life.

The subconscious works through our habits. We change our habits by first changing our thoughts. Our thoughts influence our feelings and desires which in turn lead to action. Repeated actions become habit, and habits crystallize into character. Character is the lightning rod of destiny. This process has perhaps never been summarized better than by James Allen when he gave the classic formula:

"Sow a thought, reap an action,
Sow an action, reap a habit,
Sow a habit, reap character,
Sow character, reap destiny."

Believe that your highest good is coming to you, set to work to make it so, and watch the miracle of your life unfold.

* * * * * * *

**Polishing the Jewel: Releasing the Magic of Faith**

Affirm the fact that the universe will give you exactly what you want, provided that you work with persistence, and on the condition that your goals do not infringe on the well-being and freedom of others. Develop the attitude of mind—the unbending conviction—that universal law never fails. The universe will most certainly do *its* work, if you will first do yours. Just as spring follows winter in accordance with natural laws, so will a better future come to you as you live a constructive life.

## Affirmations

*"The universe is a place of goodness, justice and grace. As I give forth out of the abundance of my heart, all good will flow to me."*

*"I am the source of my experience. A am the master of my life and the creator of my future. My world constantly gets better and more beautiful."*

*"I live in a world of magic and miracles."*

# CHAPTER NINE
## The Ninth Jewel — The Magic of Harmony

*"Don't cry, mother,"* he would answer. *"Life is paradise, and we are all in paradise, but we won't see it; if we would, we should have heaven on earth the next day."*
— Dostoyevsky, *The Brothers Karamazov*

*"We want a road map, but God hands us a musical score instead."*
— Woodene Koenig-Bricker, *365 Saints*

Underlying all seeming disturbance, imbalance, and irregularity is a world of profound harmony. The ancients called this universal harmony of living things by the name *cosmos*. The absence of order—of cosmos—was *chaos*. When you achieve harmony in yourself, you will easily grasp and express the underlying laws of the universe, for they are expressions of exquisite harmony.

This deep underlying harmony of life was perceived by Admiral Richard E. Byrd when he spent five months alone in Antarctica, near the South Pole. In his journal he described an experience that came to him one bleak and frozen night:

"I paused to listen to the silence. My breath crystallized as it passed my cheeks, drifted on a breeze gentler than a whisper. The wind vane pointed toward the South Pole. Presently the wind cups ceased their gentle turning as the cold killed the breeze. My frozen breath hung like a cloud overhead.

The day was dying, the night was being born—but with great peace. Here were the imponderable processes and forces of the cosmos, harmonious and soundless. Harmony, that was it! That was what came out of the silence—a gentle rhythm, the strain of a perfect chord, the music of the spheres, perhaps.

It was enough to catch that rhythm, momentarily to be myself a part of it. In that instant I could feel no doubt of man's oneness with the universe."

Many mystics have described the great peace and harmony that lie at the center of all apparent motion and restlessness in nature. Beyond all seeming agitation there exists this overwhelming harmony that unites and organizes all created things. Jesus called the awareness of this harmony "the peace that passes understanding."

The four elements of the ancients: fire, air, water and earth, were understood to correspond to the fundamental principles within each human being. Earth represents practicality, the capacity to get things done in physical life. Water represents the feelings and the reflective qualities of imagination. Air represents thinking, or intellect—and the ability to communicate. Fire represents the enthusiasm of our spirit and the ardor and intensity of love. The foundation of success in life is establishing harmony among these "elements" of personality, which leads to light in the mind, warmth in the feelings, and vitality in the body.

It was this meaning of the elements applied to human psychology that Shakespeare had in mind when he has Antony say of Brutus, "His life was gentle, and the elements so mixed in him that Nature might stand up and say to all the world 'This was a man!'"

Harmony is the blending of all elements in sympathetic accord. Harmony dissolves contradictions and integrates all virtues and powers. Harmony is equanimity in the life of feelings, positivity in the mind, and happiness of heart that can only spring from a loving attitude.

All of us have an impact on our environment and other people that is the result of our inner state of mind and emotions. We are constantly broadcasting our inner life into the vast etheric sea in which we are placed. All human beings are telepathic transmitters as well as receivers, like it or not. Our thoughts, moods, feelings and gestures sound a keynote—an actual vibration—which is the sum total of our personal energy field expressed as a musical tone. Although this is not perceptible to any except the most developed clairvoyants or clairaudients, it is noticed by everyone. We call it one's disposition, which is the external face of character. Your disposition is your calling card. It can be a talisman of success or a potential cause of failure.

The opposite of a harmonious disposition is a state of agitation. We all go through periods of emotional and mental agitation, but through calm breathing and awareness of our inner states, we can get a handle on our moods. Periods of quiet time set aside for reflection, prayer, or meditation are essential in establishing a habit of inner tranquillity.

Harmonious people display an evenness of temper and a gentle disposition. They wield subtle power and influence merely by their presence. People love to be around other people who have a sweet, kind temperament. The elusive, intangible element of human personality which we call *charm* is precisely a harmonious disposition. In order to acquire this psychological harmony it is helpful to focus on thoughts of peace, beauty and kindness—what Plato summed up in the motto of the philosophical ideal: goodness, beauty and truth.

Everywhere in nature we can see reciprocity or balanced exchange—what might simply be called *breathing*. It is evident in the alternation of day and night and in the rhythmic flux of the seasons. We see it in the rhythm of the tides, in the inbreath and outbreath of our lungs in respiration, and in the cycle of sleep and waking. Even the constant exchange of carbon and oxygen that exists between plants and animals is an image of this law.

Rhythmic exchange also needs to exist in our activities if we are to maintain harmony in our bodies, minds and our deeper selves. Some people tend to live mostly in their "heads," and seem to express an excessive intellectualism. Others lean towards feelings and imagination, often favoring religious or artistic pursuits. Still others live almost entirely in their bodies—in physical, sensory experience—remaining unawakened mentally and spiritually. Shakespeare poked gentle fun at this type of person in *A Midsummer Night's Dream*, when he described the workmen-turned-playwrights as "hard-handed men...who never labored in their minds 'til now."

Whatever our natural temperament or inclination, we will live more balanced and healthy lives if we find time for activities that develop all areas of our potential—thoughtful-intellectual, feeling-artistic, and physical-athletic. When we can develop a daily or weekly rhythm of living that gives expression to all these areas— thinking, feeling, and physical action—we will find that we become more harmonious as individuals. We develop "comprehensive" personalities and are less prone to illness and fatigue. We will also find that as we become more harmonious, we attune our minds more easily to our spiritual selves due to the fact that harmony is a master key that unlocks the portals of higher understanding.

Lao and Walter Russell were two individuals who lived in near perfect harmony and accord with the great laws of life. Their life together seems almost the stuff of fairy tales and dreams. They demonstrated a level of mastery and artistry in living that is truly rare.

Walter Russell, whose faith in the universal laws was described in Chapter Eight, was a true modern "Renaissance man." He was an accomplished musician, architect, philosopher, and scientist. He is also one of the few individuals to demonstrate virtuosity in both painting and sculpture. Not until after his fiftieth birthday did he take up the study of science, yet through his extraordinary penetration into the nature of matter and the spiritual laws behind the visible universe, he was able to discover two new elements— neptunium and plutonium—before the rest of the scientific world acknowledged their existence. Yet he never studied physics, had almost no formal schooling, and read only a few books in his entire life. Walter Russell's knowledge came through direct experience and what we might call "revelation." His scientific masterpiece, *The Universal One*, was known to sell for thousands of dollars after it had gone out of print.

He and Lao Russell first "met" when they spoke by phone.

They recognized instantly the depth of their connection. Walter Russell caught an immediate flight to meet the woman who was to become his wife. Their harmonious life together was a demonstration of the principle of rhythmic, balanced exchange. As they eloquently expressed in words—and lived even more eloquently— happiness in a relationship can only come when each partner seeks first to give happiness to the other. The "art of relationship" is mastered when giving and receiving—or as they would say, giving and *regiving*—becomes a balanced interplay of loving exchanges on all levels: physical, emotional, mental and spiritual. In their own words, "what you do to your neighbor is the most important event of every moment."

In 1948 they acquired a marble Renaissance palace on a Virginia mountaintop. Today their beautiful home, named Swannanoa, is often open to the public. It is graced with many of Mr. Russell's world-renowned paintings and sculptures. They founded a correspondence school called the University of Science and Philosophy. Together they wrote a year-long study course on the principles of universal law. This course has been sent to students throughout the world and has changed the lives of thousands of people. They themselves said that each sentence of this lengthy course was written by each of them together.

I had the good fortune of meeting Lao Russell at Swannanoa briefly on two visits to their beautiful home. Once in her presence, I knew that I was meeting a living saint. Although quite elderly at the time, she was vital and energetic. Her voice had a remarkable resonant quality and she emanated extraordinary gentleness and love. She is one of the few people around whom I have seen a brilliant field of light. She expressed words to me that I will never forget. "In awareness of your God-light is your greatest happiness and the fulfillment of your purpose on earth." And on another occasion: "Love will touch your heart and soul because you express love!"

One of the greatest challenges facing all human beings is to establish harmony in relationships. Intimate relationships are a primary "testing ground" for the law of harmony. The experiences of family and partnerships are "basic training"—the "boot camp" everybody has to pass through. Earth is a school of relationships that goes from "kindergarten to graduate school." Everyone has lessons to learn and tests to pass. Few there are who haven't flunked at least a few exams in "Relationship U." It isn't surprising that relationships have been called the "last frontier." To achieve harmony in an intimate relationship, it is true that both partners must be able to express their individuality and be free individuals within the partnership. But the main requirement is mutual concern for each other's well-being and happiness, which finds expression through acts of kindness, assistance, and generosity.

Social harmony among people produces a healthy circulation of "life force" in a group, whether it be a family, a business, or a larger institution. This implies that the gifts of all individuals find expression in the community, and that the well-being of the community is considered by every individual. This doesn't mean there aren't problems, but that there is an attitude of goodwill that promotes resolution of conflicts and misunderstandings. Lines of communication stay open and feelings are expressed constructively. The attitude that leads to harmony includes an active interest in the well-being of others, along with respect for the rights and liberties of individuals.

As all musicians and music lovers know, rhythm is an element of harmony. For harmony to exist in a relationship, there needs to be a rhythm—a balanced interplay—to the interactions between partners. Put simply, each partner must learn to give, receive, and then give back. Attentive listening is vital to this process. By living in accordance with this principle of harmonious giving and receiving, tensions and resentments do not build to the breaking point. If one partner does most of the giving, the relationship is out of balance and unhealthy.

Successful relationships are built on the foundation of reciprocity—of rhythmic balanced interchange between partners. Without kindness, harmony in relationships cannot exist. In order to experience love, one must give love. The principle of reciprocal giving must be firmly established if relationships are to be healthy and happy.

An intimate relationship is not a business agreement or a bargaining process, nor is it a field of negotiation where each side tries to get the upper hand. First and foremost, it is a friendship. Only friendship can give long-term staying power to a relationship. Emerson said that a friend is the highest product of evolution. The foundation for friendship is a sharing of values—a harmony of viewpoint. In relationships of all kinds, a sense of humor can do wonders in maintaining harmony.

A marvelous story from the Brother's Grimm illustrates the power of laughter. A young simpleton is given a golden goose by a little gray man with whom he has shared his lunch. A young woman, thinking to steal a golden feather from the goose, becomes stuck fast to the bird as soon as she touches it. Her sisters in turn become latched on to her, and soon there is a whole row of people stuck one to the other in a line, following behind the simpleton. The zany procession arrives at the castle of a princess so somber she has never laughed in her life. The king has promised his daughter in marriage to the first man who can make her laugh. When the princess sees the parade of people stuck fast to the simpleton's golden goose, she breaks out in hilarious laughter, as if she would never stop. The simpleton marries the princess and becomes heir to the kingdom; they live together happily for many years.

Humor helps free the soul, symbolized by the princess in the story. This leads to the alchemical marriage, the harmonious union of our soul with our Higher Self. As a result, we inherit the kingdom of happiness. Through laughter, we open ourselves to the lightness of life. Humor dispels darkness. Laughter is a universal language of the heart that everyone understands. There is a wisdom in laughter that goes beyond words.

Another area where harmony is crucial is that of health. Disease is a symptom of imbalance in the organism and the personality. Health is a sign of harmony. Many people think of illness as the cause of their problems. In fact, illness and disease are the organism's effort to heal itself of disharmony. What we call illness is actually a cure. Pain is the body's way of warning us something is wrong. Pain is not the source of the problem, neither are symptoms the problem. The cause lies elsewhere, often in the realm of erroneous thoughts, misplaced beliefs, or hardened emotions. It does no good to blame—either ourselves or anyone else. Healing begins with acceptance.

There are many mysteries to illness that we do not fully understand. There are cases where the person seems to be doing everything "right," and yet they still suffer. They are living a constructive life, eating healthy foods, and expanding themselves spiritually. Despite this, they cannot seem to eliminate their illness.

The causes of illness often are deeply hidden. The very last thing we should do is to stand in judgment—of ourselves or of others. Illness often teaches us what nothing else can. Poor health or a bout with illness can often dramatically change one's life, opening the doors to a larger reality. Health difficulties teach important life lessons and can challenge us to unlock the deeper powers of the self. Our power to heal ourselves is closely linked with the spiritual power of our higher nature—a power which can perform miracles in every area of life. The inner exertion and effort of soul that is often required to overcome or live with an illness may be likened to a spiritual transformation or "conversion" that leaves one permanently changed. The life-altering power of illness can have a redemptive quality and can be liberating if one is open to the lessons that come through the healing process. Illness is one of life's greatest teachers; disease can be a most potent, albeit drastic, medicine of the soul. More than one person has said, "My illness saved my life."

An example of the power of illness to trigger a life-changing transformation comes from the remarkable experience of Greg Anderson. In 1984 he was diagnosed with lung cancer and told that he had thirty days to live. Not only did he respond to this "death sentence" by healing himself without the aid of conventional medicine, but through his best-selling books he has taught thousands of people the laws of healing and wellness that he discovered in the process. Greg says healing and wellness begin with developing a love affair with life—"shifting our awareness to look for the joys that come in small, precious packages."

Illness can be a stimulus to growth. It is a call for harmony. If any part of the body is ill, one must seek the cure in the health and harmony of the whole organism, the whole human being. Poor health is a call for the restoring of order and harmony in one's thoughts, feelings, words and deeds. The cure for illness can be found in the way one lives.

A woman I knew in California applied these truths of healing and became a "walking miracle" as a result. She was legally blind and confined to a wheelchair due to a partial paralysis of her legs. A year and a half later she was fit and active, licensed to drive a car, an avid outdoorswoman, and a book enthusiast. The only sign of her former paralysis was a slight limp. She still wore thick glasses and had to wear sunglasses outdoors, but in most respects she was completely healthy and "normal." What accounted for the "miracle?" First of all, she had an intense desire to heal herself. She enrolled in many personal growth classes and applied the principles of right thinking, forgiveness of self and others, positive affirmation, and faith in the beneficent laws of life. She radically altered her diet, became a vegetarian, ate pure and wholesome "living foods," and surrounded herself with loving and supportive friends. She herself said often, "If I can do this, anyone can." When we approach life with the right consciousness and a constructive attitude, miracles of healing are possible.

It is becoming more widely accepted today that inner states of feeling and thought are reflected in the outer disposition of the body. But it is also true that we can change our moods and our health by altering our posture and bodily gestures. You can change your mood for the better by "acting as if" you are in a happy, healthy frame of mind. Simply by smiling we can improve our psychological state. William James, one of America's greatest philosophers and psychologists, said that "It is physically impossible to remain blue and depressed while acting out symptoms of being radiantly happy."

Sorrow and fear cause the blood vessels to contract. This restriction of the arteries leads to loss of energy and physical apathy. Because our cells and organs do not receive the blood they need, we become tired and listless. In the long run, this leads to poor health. The antidote is not drugs and medication, but an inner change in attitude. When we restore harmony to our feelings and thoughts, we increase the flow of vital energy to our physical organs.

Strive to begin each day on a positive note. Wake up and stretch and speak affirmations aloud. Tell the world you love it. Affirm your unity with life. Laugh out loud and tell yourself what a wonderful being you are. Establish your connection with the universal life. That means to feel it!

Self-acceptance plays an important role in health and harmonious living. But the idea can be ambiguous. Self-acceptance doesn't mean becoming lazy in the face of personal shortcomings, or "throwing in the towel" when it comes to making life changes. Virtually all of us have areas in which we can improve. We are "diamonds in the rough" that need polishing and refinement to enhance our inner beauty. Passive acceptance of personal weakness is self-defeating. Paraphrasing the old adage, wisdom implies knowing the difference between what we can change and what we can't.

The other side of the coin is that people have a tendency to be needlessly self-critical and unhappy with themselves. This can undermine one's self-image and health. A hair-cutter once told me that nearly all of her customers with straight hair wished they had curly or wavy hair. Virtually all of her customers with wavy or curly hair wished their hair was straight. Similarly, anorexic girls see themselves as "overweight" regardless of how thin they become. We seem to have an inherent dissatisfaction about our appearance. Much of this comes from the commercial culture's immature obsession with external beauty.

Personal dissatisfaction on the "soul level"—the level of attitudes and emotions—becomes constructive when it spurs us to become wiser, stronger, and more loving. A "divine discontent" that urges us towards self-improvement is a good thing. Self-acceptance means the recognition and acceptance of our true essence. In the best sense, self-acceptance implies embracing the light, love and goodness of our deeper self. When we can love ourselves for the beauty of our "hidden splendor," not egotistically but out of joyous acceptance of our intrinsic nature, we open the "windows of our soul." That's why it's been said that "Enlightenment is falling in love with yourself for the first time."

Laughter plays a harmonizing role in healing of the body and the soul as well as in relationships. Even the four temperaments of medieval medicine—based on the ancient Greek practices codified by Hippocrates—were linked to four particular body fluids, called *humors*. The predominance of a specific fluid, or humour, resulted in a person's essential temperament, or disposition. This indicates that the origin of the word *humor* is itself related to the idea of health, which implies a harmonious balance among all bodily and psychological functions. When we laugh, we open ourselves to the influence of harmony. Laughter heals the soul as well as the body.

It is important to realize we cannot achieve harmony in ourselves if we continue to cause suffering to other beings. It is of great consequence how we treat the animals as well as our fellow humans. If our thoughts and behavior cause suffering, we will feel the backlash. One day in the near future, the elimination of suffering—insofar as it is humanly possible—and the cruelty that leads to suffering, will become a central motivation in the lives of a significant portion of humankind. Through the study of the laws implicit in nature, one inevitably arrives at the following basic maxim: in order to eliminate harm from one's own life, cause no harm to others.

It is essential to live one's life at the origin of experience, that is, at the point of cause. Archimedes said "give me a lever and fulcrum and I will move the world." We all possess these tools. The fulcrum is our minds, which we can use to select the kind of experience we desire. The lever is the ability to consciously act in accordance with universal laws and principles. A simple way to express this is that "You get what you set." We can remove obstacles from our path, just as a lever and fulcrum can remove a large boulder, if we understand these truths.

Our thoughts are the magnets which draw experience to us. We can set ourselves up for success or failure by our customary attitude of mind. If we set in motion constructive forces through our thoughts, actions and words—forces that benefit and uplift— the effects will take care of themselves. If we apply the mighty laws of balance and reciprocity through our inner attitude of love and goodwill, we will start to create harmony in our lives, our health, and our relationships.

To live in harmony means to live at peace with ourselves and the world. Living in peace implies accepting the differences of all people in the world. Every human being expresses a unique pattern that is a necessary part of the whole texture of life. Each of us is a strand in the universal tapestry. All human beings weave a singular thread in the universal pattern.

A world of infinite peace surrounds the earth and all creation.

Peace in the soul begins when we can embrace the world with love in our hearts.

********

**Polishing the Jewel: Releasing the Magic of Harmony**

Activity # one:

Upon waking in the morning laugh loudly and heartily. Then say aloud and with conviction, "I feel great!" It may take practice to really be able to laugh and affirm these words with enthusiasm and with *feeling*. Keep trying! Do this every day for at least a month and you may never want to stop.

Activity # two:

Picture a triangle with sides of equal length—an equilateral triangle. Draw this triangle on paper. Write your name in the center of the triangle. At one of the corners write the word *thinking*, at another corner write *feeling*, at the third corner write the word *action*. Realize that the triangle represents your own three-fold personality. Each angle represents one of the three "soul forces" which energize all human beings. Most likely, one of the three will be dominant in your personality, and one will be less developed than the other two. You will tend to emphasize either thinking, feeling or action.

Think of activities and devise a weekly plan to help you balance your triangle. For instance, if you are less developed in the area of emotions or feeling, you might want to enhance your artistic sense and your appreciation of beauty and esthetics. Perhaps you could visit local art galleries, or see some live theater. Or you might want to explore the music of some of the great composers.

Best of all, take up an artistic pursuit, such as learning to play a musical instrument, or taking classes in painting or drawing. If you are very active in your mind, but tend to be physically sedentary, make a point to take regular walks (in nature, if possible), work out at the gym, ride a bicycle, or become active in a movement or dance group. If you are predominantly a feeling person—or if you are "short on words, but long on deeds"—you may want to exercise your intellect. In this case, begin to read some of the classics of literature, or the works of great philosophers. The reading list at the end of this book would also be a good starting point. Reading the world's finest poetry is an excellent way to enhance both the feeling and the thinking points of your triangle. Astonish your friends with your newly ripened wisdom!

Recognize that these three forces of thought, feeling, and will are reflections of the attributes traditionally associated with divinity: wisdom, love, and strength. As we introduce harmony and balance into our lives, we will become more capable of expressing these higher qualities. They make their appearance in our personalities as intelligence and light in our thinking, warmth and kindness in our feelings, and in the ability to act swiftly, effectively and decisively.

When you make the effort to develop yourself as a balanced, harmonious individual, you stir unseen forces that come to your aid. Who knows? Perhaps one day the angels themselves will begin to whisper to you their secrets.

## Affirmations

*"I live in a world of perfect harmony. My mind and heart are at peace."*

*"I develop a harmonious disposition by holding luminous and loving thoughts in my mind."*

*"All events and all people are working together harmoniously to help me achieve my goals."*

*"May the light of wisdom stream through my thinking, may warmth and kindness flow through my feelings, and may strength of will characterize my every deed."*

# CHAPTER TEN
## The Tenth Jewel — The Magic of Prosperity

*"Success is a journey, not a destination."* — Wayne Dyer

*"Seek and you shall find. Ask and you shall receive. Knock and it shall be opened unto you."* — Jesus

There exists in the universe a limitless source of all good things. Life is an inexhaustible cornucopia of energy, substance, and variety. Limitations do not exist in the universal mind that underlies creation. Limitation exists only in human thinking.

The law of abundance is not a carefully guarded mystery. It is an open secret. All human beings have the capacity to become prosperous through the right use of their faculties. A simple bar magnet is useful to illustrate one of the essential principles of prosperity.

If a magnet is struck a heavy blow with a hammer, the tiny iron atoms are shaken out of alignment and the magnet loses its drawing power. By stroking the iron again with the end of another magnet, the microscopic iron crystals will realign and the full force of the magnet returns.

All of us have a "prosperity magnet" within ourselves. With many people it has become "demagnetized" due to the heavy blows of life—or as a result of the destructive impact of discordant thinking and emotion. A sure way to weaken your prosperity magnet is through fear and negative thinking. Fortunately, regardless of the condition of your "magnet," you can restore its full attractive power. When your thoughts become positive, you align the "crystal atoms" of your mental magnet in one direction. Automatically you will begin to pull to yourself the resources you require. Not only is it necessary to overcome habitual negativity in order to improve as a person, but one's ability to prosper is also largely dependent on replacing a negative trend of thought and feeling with an overwhelmingly positive one.

When I was teaching at a small private school in northern California, I was on the "tuition assistance committee," which worked with parents who could not afford the school's full tuition. The school had a fund to help these families. In return for the assistance, the parents were expected to "volunteer" their services by performing tasks such as class-room cleanup and grounds maintenance, which would help the school by reducing costs. There was one woman, a parent, who was always complaining about how tough her life was and how difficult things were financially, and yet she almost never showed up to perform the tasks that were her responsibility as part of the tuition-assistance agreement. It seemed to a couple of us that she needed a dose of prosperity thinking to reverse her attitude. So we decided to send her a copy of Catherine Ponder's book, *The Dynamic Laws of Prosperity*. Inside the cover we placed a crisp new twenty dollar bill, then mailed the book to her anonymously. The change was gradual but dramatic. She was quiet for a few weeks, but the complaints stopped. Soon she was performing her tasks cheerfully, even offering advice to other parents receiving tuition assistance. This little incident also demonstrates the power of anonymous giving to change people's lives.

The sun is constantly demonstrating an essential law of prosperity. This "day star" may be described as a repository of cosmic treasures in the form of light, warmth, and radiant substance. The sun is blessed with all these treasures because it gives ceaselessly of itself. If the sun produced only enough light and warmth for itself alone, our very earth could not exist. This radiant orb is an image of a basic truth of life—that those who give, prosper. Like the sun, successful people learn to produce a shining surplus. They open up a channel of helpfulness that transcends purely personal needs. When we become like the sun, a source of abundance and blessing, our life becomes enriched.

Prosperity begins in the workshop of our minds, where the architect within us draws up the master plan. The blueprint of your personal economic conditions is created in your thinking process. Positive mind-images create positive circumstances.

Many people have small goals and limited expectations. Life provides for them in accordance with what they expect and request. If you want more out of life, increase your expectations, and be prepared to back up your demands with personal effort. Life will give us what we ask of it, provided that we perform useful service to back up our desires.

The remarkable American teacher, Peter Rosen, demonstrates a seemingly effortless mastery of the laws of prosperity. In the delightul and inspiring book by John Roberts, entitled *The Fruit of Your Thoughts*, he paraphrases Peter as follows:

> "Give what you have in complete faith that if you contribute to life then life will return the bounty... You only

attain wealth in the long run by enriching the lives of others first. This is the law of enrichment. The universe rewards you when you are a faithful steward. It is a spiritual law that when you serve and enrich others by bringing beauty, joy and comfort into their lives, an abundance of time, money, health and prosperity will seek you out."

The basis of economic life lies in supplying needed goods and in providing beneficial services. By opening up a channel of helpfulness we make it possible to receive benefits. Here again we come to the conclusion that the fundamental economic law is the law of the seed. As you sow, you shall reap. If you sow radishes, you won't reap roses.

Just as you cannot harvest what you have not planted, you can only extract from your life what you have put into it. The fruits of our labors are in direct proportion to the seeds invested through our activities. The law is always just. As you act, the universe responds. What you draw into your life is inseparably connected to the forces you have triggered in motion by the manner in which you have lived from the dawn of your existence. Regardless of where you are now financially, your conditions will improve if you live to serve constructively as a matter of personal life policy.

When you release energy in service, you establish a cause which will result in a definite effect. This effect is first felt in the lives of those whom your service benefits. But the eventual result will be a return of energy as a reciprocal force that impacts you and your living circumstances. In other words, when you give of yourself you are making deposits in the "vaults of heaven," your divine bank account. In times of need you will have something on which to draw. The act of giving results in receiving. Your income—and the status of your personal economy—in the long run rests entirely in your own hands and in your own mind.

My friend, Ricardo, and I were once talking about the laws of prosperity. One of his favorite words was *abundance*. He told me that it came from the Latin root, *abundare*, which can be translated as meaning, "to make waves." This is enlightening when we consider the modern view of quantum physics that sees the material universe as an ocean of light-wave frequencies of varying modulations and "densities." Becoming prosperous and abundant means to make waves, the right kind of waves. The right kind of "waves" are those that benefit, help, assist and prosper. The universe is a gigantic sounding board that will send back to us what we send out into the world, often enhanced and multiplied many times. I knew a man who had a great expression for this truth. His advice—paraphrasing scripture—was to "throw your bread upon the waters and it will come back fruitcake."

Although most of us have not reached a point where we can directly manifest from the ethers with a wave of our hands, many spiritual leaders and saints demonstrate that the concept of a "struggle for existence" is an illusion. Thousands of people have witnessed Sai Baba, the great Indian spiritual leader, materialize rings, food and many other things seemingly "out of the air." If we express good in all that we do, the universe provides for us. Many people who have made spiritual goals a priority find that material things come to them more easily. This is one of the meanings of Christ's words, "seek first the Kingdom of Heaven and all these things will be added unto you." "All these things" refer to the normal wishes and aspirations of most people: material security, fulfilling work, friendship, a successful intimate relationship. When we organize our life so that seeking spiritual enlightenment—"treasures in Heaven"—becomes a priority, other areas of life start to fall into place as if by magic. Once your life has an influence that spreads beyond purely personal gain, the floodgates of universal supply are flung open. This means creating an avenue of service that goes beyond the satisfaction of purely selfish interests.

Consider the moral and ethical implications of your economic activities in the light of the law of reciprocal exchange. What kind of future are you creating for yourself? Be sure that your professional activities are truly constructive and life-affirming. If your current employment is destructive or less than ethical, ask yourself why you are there. If your work truly provides benefits to others, do it with enthusiasm, to the very best of your ability.

Many people, particularly if they are an "employee," work with a listless attitude, holding back their best, as if they are really meant for better things than the work currently before them. Such an approach is self-defeating. In reality, everyone is self-employed, no matter who signs their paycheck. New and better possibilities will only open up if you give your best in your present work. No matter what your current employment or financial circumstances, if you work with energy, kindness and enthusiasm—performing service to the best of your ability—you will prosper.

Many people short-circuit the good effects of their constructive efforts by mixing them with many negative, destructive seeds. Some people live a lifestyle far exceeding their income. They pile up debts which become a mountain they have to surmount in order to reach stable prosperity. Those who receive benefits without reciprocating for what they receive, build up a debt in their cosmic treasury account. The backlash effect of the causation principle insures that even what they appear to have will eventually be taken from them. Cosmic law demands that the piper be paid.

During the past several decades there has been a tremendous expansion of the "lottery mentality." Governments have promoted this way of thinking in order to expand their revenue base; most states now have a lottery. More and more people are staking their future prosperity on buying the winning ticket, or getting rich with a "lucky strike" in the casinos. This is a disturbing trend, for it indicates a lack of understanding of the fundamental law of life, the law of the seed. The law of causation decrees that you can't get something for nothing. Only service produces affluence. Only *your* service can increase *your* personal affluence. People would begin to expand their personal prosperity by diverting the money they might throw away in the mad chase for the elusive lottery jackpot and instead gave it away to charitable organizations or to people in financial need. America today is full of such needy people. When you give, you invest in your own future. Gambling is not an investment, it's a form of taxation.

In most people's minds, money is equated with prosperity. The reason for this is obvious, for money is needed to purchase goods and services and is the central means of financial power in today's world. But many people make money the primary focus and objective of their career efforts, which is a fundamental error in approach. Money is not the *source* of affluence and prosperity, it is a *result* of services performed and benefits created. "Money," said the Roman philosopher Seneca, "has never yet made anyone rich."

Strictly speaking, money is not wealth—nor is it the source of wealth. Real *wealth*—as distinguished from *money*—implies generosity of mind, heart, and character. Gold has always been a symbol of the spirit, the immortal divine spark, the true source of all wealth. When one is inwardly wealthy—in terms of character, attitude, and soul qualities—external abundance will also appear. If one creates the right inner conditions, material wealth will manifest. Among the most important of these inner characteristics are a positive attitude, gratefulness for life experiences, a harmonious disposition, and the ability to enjoy both solitude and the company of other people.

The true function of money is as a medium of exchange. Money *represents* value that has been created by goods produced or services performed. Essentially, money is a symbol of the universal life force that permeates all things and which is, for all practical purposes, limitless and infinite. When we live a constructive life, money—representing the life force—automatically flows in our direction, so long as we do not obstruct this flow by selfishness and by negative thinking and action. We tap the cosmic treasury of universal abundance by the attitude that realizes there is no lack in the spiritual or material universe. To this opulent attitude of consciousness must be added a constructive lifestyle. A basic criterion of prosperity is to work positively in whatever field of service one chooses. Abundance lies in constructive employment of talents and abilities. When you give your best in service, benefits will accrue in direct proportion to your helpful efforts. Money always tends to flow in the direction of activity and energy, so long as these are positive. Enterprise and initiative designed to provide assistance to others will always lead to financial rewards.

Unfortunately, our modern economic life is burdened by a tremendous distortion, which is the result of our currency being created out of nothing, and issued as debt. There is nothing tangible to back up the "money"—that is, the *debt*—that is issued by our central bank and the large commercial banks. This leads to inflation and the centralization of financial power in the hands of a few.

Compound interest, when applied to personal indebtedness, becomes an all-consuming monster that can bring about financial ruin. Many psychological and health problems—as well as tensions in relationships—are related to the trauma and difficulty of getting out of debt. I saw a bumper sticker that reflected this fact. It read: "I don't need therapy. I need money!" The debt system is insidious because *everyone* is made to over-exert just to keep up with payments. It has been estimated that as much as fifty percent of all bills paid—including those paid by individuals who have no debt of their own—goes to the service of corporate debt. (Not to mention the federal government debt) The commercial propaganda of the corporate and financial institutions has brainwashed an entire culture to embrace a lifestyle of living beyond one's means. In the future, this system will be reformed, which will lead to universal prosperity and abundance on a scale never before experienced on earth.

Even with the current distortions in our economy, we can build the foundation for an abundant life right now. We can prosper despite the present flaws in our system. Two keys are essential. First, plug into the limitless universal storehouse of all good things by a positive life outlook and an unwavering faith in the overwhelming goodness of the universal laws. Secondly, live a positive and constructive life, in thought and gesture, remembering to stay out of debt insofar as is possible.

Another ancient prosperity principle is that of proportional giving, known as tithing. When you give a portion of your income to organizations which work to make the world a better place, you align yourself with the advancing momentum of life itself. Your efforts become linked with the divine force which is drawing all things towards a higher state of being. By pledging a proportion of all your earnings to further the objectives of the divine world order, you build your life on a firm foundation.

The word "tithe" comes from the Anglo-Saxon word, *tethoa*, which means "a tenth." The tithe is traditionally ten percent of earned income, though you can start with a smaller percent and work up to that. Some individuals give even more than ten percent. The important thing to consider in tithing is that a portion of the fruits of your labor flows to organizations that are truly worthy. These can be any spiritual or charitable institutions that are uplifting humanity, relieving the suffering in the world, and whose philosophy is in accordance with the beneficent laws of the universe.

John Templeton is a man of humble origins who grew up on a poor Tennessee farm. As a result of living in accordance with the deeper laws, he has become one of the world's wealthiest men and a noted philanthropist. The famous family of mutual funds that bears his name is one of the most successful and respected of all investment companies. In his inspiring book entitled, *Discovering the Laws of Life*, he notes that, "In my lifetime of observing many hundreds of families, almost without exception, the family which tithes for more than ten years becomes both prosperous and happy. This is the one investment suitable for all persons." Tithing is an investment in your future which will help you to establish financial security in your life.

To improve your finances and increase your prosperity, begin now to more effectively serve those with whom you come in contact. Initiate a method of constructive service which goes beyond your personal needs only. Every helpful act, every beneficial deed, carries the seed of its own return. Your financial condition and the environment in which you live are the result of all that you have ever thought, felt, said and done. You will draw to yourself the very conditions you focus on mentally, for like attracts like.

You may have whatever you desire if you are willing to pay the price in energy expended through effort and service. You reach the place in life where you begin to receive what you desire when you can picture yourself having what you want. But you must first set the necessary energy in motion that will bring you what you have earned. You have to "make waves." These "waves" are created through luminous frequencies of inspired thought and loving feelings, and by engaging in constructive actions. Keep in mind that "service" can be anything of a helpful, beneficial nature. It is well to remember that you can't give what you don't have, and you only have what you have earned through meaningful use of talents.

When you work with a feeling of love and gratitude—out of a desire to assist others—you may be sure the rewards will take care of themselves. You hold in your hands the key to a more prosperous life.

\*\*\*\*\*\*\*

## Polishing the Jewel: Releasing the Magic of Prosperity

Activity # one

An excellent means of enhancing your level of prosperity and increasing your success consciousness is by keeping a diary for this purpose. Divide each page in half down the middle, creating two columns. Title the left column "gifts and services," the right column "miracles and manifestations." At the end of each day note down in the left column all your kind, helpful actions and gifts. This could be almost any constructive act: giving flowers, sending a greeting card, donating money or clothing to a homeless person, volunteering your time. Possibilities are endless. The other column is for the miracles and benefits that begin to flow into your life. The left hand column is outflow, the right hand column is inflow. Make an entry each day. If you persist with positive efforts and seek to expand your givingness, you will be amazed and delighted at the increasing abundance and "miracles" that begin to flow to you. When you combine this with affirmations and visualizing the achieving of your goals, you can transform your life. To be truly effective you must work this plan for at least ninety days. You may want to keep this little "book of miracles" as a permanent part of your inner and outer work.

Activity # two

Many people block the circulation of abundance into their lives by accumulating vast amounts of material things that they no longer need or use. Make a thorough inventory of all your material possessions. Decide which ones are just taking up space, or no longer serve you. Resolve to move them out of your life! Have a garage sale of these items. If you can't sell them, give them away. There is a saying in India that, "What isn't given is lost." Remember that giving opens the way for receiving.

<u>Activity # three</u>

Sit down in your favorite chair with a pad of paper and a pen in your hands. Reflect on your long-term life goals. What would you most like to do with your life? Ask yourself if your work or career is really helping to make the world a better place. If not, why not? In the light of the law of the seed, consider the long term implications of engaging in your present vocation.

Many people would like to change their work or their profession, but are not able to do so, for numerous valid reasons. Even if your work is not your ideal, think of activities you can engage in that will help create a better world.

## Affirmations

*"I hold the key to limitless abundance by the constructive use of my mind and all my faculties."*

*"As I benefit others through service, I open a channel of abundance to flow into my life."*

*"There are no limitations in universal mind. I affirm abundance and prosperity for myself and others."*

*"All that I need and more is coming my way."*

# CHAPTER ELEVEN
# The Eleventh Jewel — The Magic of Inner Unfolding

*"I shall endeavor now to make the divine in me arise and meet the divine in the universe."*
— Plotinus

*"At the still-point in the center of the circle one can see the infinite in all things."*
— Chuang Tsu

*"...a deeper knowledge of universal laws is contingent upon a deeper knowledge of the self."*
— Lawrence Blair

All of life is a development, a progression, an unfolding. Our life on earth is a series of lessons that lead to maturity—the growth of our soul and spirit. The earth is a school and all individuals will find themselves drawn to the classroom appropriate for the lessons they need. We always attract the exact combination of elements which help us take the next step in our growth. Our teachers are everywhere. We find them in the challenges and opportunities life brings us—the people we meet, and the discoveries we make.

Our souls are unfolding in the manner of a flower, each petal revealing a different facet of our nature. The lotus is an ancient symbol of the soul's growth because it is an emblem which reflects the human condition. Out of the mud the shoot extends upward, pushing through murky water until it reaches the clear water near the top of the pond. Finally it bursts forth into the pure air and blossoms radiantly beneath the brilliant beams of the sun. The lotus is a picture of the soul that must grow through experiences of earth (physical experience), water (the emotional life), and air (intellectual experience)—finally blossoming into maturity under the influence of our divine spirit, represented by the sun.

We all live in the universal ocean of life—a complex field of energies, elements and forces. By the law of affinity we draw to ourselves the elements that exactly correspond to the nature of our thoughts, feelings and deeds. Just as a fish absorbs from the water precisely the minerals and particles that correspond exactly to its nature, so does each human being attract what it needs from the great etheric ocean of life. If we change our "nature," that is, the qualities of our inner world of thought, feeling, moods and imagination, we change the flow of materials which we attract. Every impulse toward a better life instantly releases the elements one needs from the universal mind. When we send out a thought of love—a vibration from our heart—the heart of the universe responds.

Spiritual unfolding is a process of transformation and enlightenment. We grow from darkness toward light, from ignorance to wisdom, from frustration to fulfillment. The American spiritual teacher, Gangaji, gently reminds us that we are already free. Who we are, essentially, has always been awake and enlightened. But we must discover this essence—the truth of our being. We must have that experience of illumination, that blazing self-recognition that transforms us.

Why is it that so few people have this experience, even among experienced meditators and those who have spent years on the spiritual path? Perhaps it is because we have not created the appropriate conditions for enlightenment to occur. Illumination itself takes place in an instant of serene self-remembrance, but we must create the conditions for this to happen. Creating those conditions is a process that evolves through time in the manner of a plant unfolding. A newly planted rose seed does not blossom into a fully formed rose over night.

In the ancient Greek myth of Demeter, the goddess of nature, she told the people to build a temple in her honor so that she might come and dwell on earth. Our higher divine nature also needs a "temple" in which to live. We ourselves become the temple. We build the temple of our enlightenment by transforming our personalities—that is, our thoughts, feelings, and our power to act. The tools we use are light, love, and truth.

Alchemical texts speak of "fixing the volatile," which refers to capturing the life force, or "energy essence," of the divine spark. One of the great epics of western spirituality is the story of Parzival, the young knight who went in quest of the Grail—the legendary cup that caught the blood of Christ at the crucifixion. The Grail represents the chalice our souls create in order to hold the energies of enlightenment, the frequencies of our Higher Self. The spirit is mighty, beautiful, joyous and free. It is stifled if instead of a temple it has only a "dusty hovel or a ramshackle ruin." As we expand the light in our minds and the love in our hearts, our souls become living temples—capable of expressing the magnitude of our spiritual essence. The path of inner unfolding is the path of "discovering" the Grail. Actually the Grail is not so much *found* as it is *fashioned*. We fashion our grail chalice when we forge our minds and hearts into vessels fit to hold the immortal essence of the divine spark. We most easily accomplish this by living in attunement with the universal laws.

Perhaps the most perfect symbol of the soul's metamorphosis is the butterfly. The lowly caterpillar devours living things, leaving a trail of waste and destruction—the hallmark of a true pest. Then some mysterious urge prompts it to wrap itself in a fine substance which it produces from within itself—a substance that it weaves from out of its own hidden powers. Within the secret world of the cocoon it undergoes a miraculous development, emerging in time as an entirely new creature, utterly different from the caterpillar it once was. Not only is the butterfly a marvel of grace and beauty—seemingly a winged flower—but it is beneficial as well, for it serves to pollinate many plants, giving life to future generations.

The butterfly is nature's eternal emblem of the human soul. Within the human heart is an urge to grow out of the ugly stage of "caterpillar"—the greedy, destructive pest—and become a creature of beauty and grace. Beyond that, the butterfly teaches us that it is possible to grow wings, speaking symbolically, and fly. This beautiful creature is the promise of our happy future. The butterfly is a symbol of the soul that emerges from the darkness of ignorance and sorrow and is reborn into the light of higher truth. Many of us still "crawl on our stomachs," ravaging our way through life, leaving a trail of destruction in our wake. If you aspire to become like a butterfly, you have to stop living like a caterpillar.

There exist in all human beings dormant qualities that, when awakened, will grant us higher perception—direct vision of spiritual truth. We all have the capacity to become conscious in the spiritual dimensions—to be reborn onto higher planes of existence. The means to awaken these slumbering organs of enlightenment is by a transformation of the forces of thinking and feeling.

For this reason thinking and feeling should be considered sacred processes and deserve our full attention. The time-honored methods of prayer, meditation and contemplation are means to transform thinking and feeling, and to unfold the qualities of our inner self. Prayer and meditation elevate our consciousness and put us in touch with forces, elements and beings which heal and transform. They represent a higher form of breathing—a reciprocal give and take with the divine atmosphere of a higher world of which our souls and spirits are a part.

The inner activity of the caterpillar in the cocoon represents prayer, meditation, contemplation and study. These sacred inner processes enable us to build a bridge of light—a rainbow bridge—constructed of our best feelings, ideas, hopes and aspirations. This bridge of consciousness links us with the celestial regions from which our spirit has descended to earth. From this higher region come intuition and guidance for life—creative ideas that inspire us to act in heroic ways.

Regardless of whether we call it God, Christ, the Buddha Nature, the Absolute, *Atma*, the Supreme or Universal Consciousness, there is a fountain of radiant light within each soul. Contact with this center of our being brings joy and strength for life. This is the source of wisdom, love and power—the imprisoned splendor that awaits release.

One of the first teachers I had was an Indonesian Buddhist named Tom, who worked for a large multinational corporation. As a young man he had healed himself of a severe illness by meditation, breathing exercises, and yoga. One of the things that impressed me most about him, in addition to his gentleness and unassuming manner, was his extraordinary power of concentration. He told me that it was good to read books on spiritual subjects, but advised that they could only take one so far. Nothing could take the place of experience.

Actual spiritual experience can only come as a result of *living* the truths, and by the practice of meditation and prayer. A person lacking experience in spiritual matters is like someone who has read dozens of books about Mozart, and knows almost everything about his life, but has never actually heard his music. Only when you have heard his music will you know the greatness of Mozart. Similarly, only through expanding your inner life through periods of contemplation will you begin to experience the bright energy of the indwelling spark.

Many people who become interested in spiritual matters find it difficult to shake the materialistic bias of our culture. They would like to believe in the reality of the "higher worlds," but can't seem to do it. If one practices meditation for a long period of time, the conviction will gradually arise as a result of inner experience that the spiritual world is more authentic, because more enduring, than the physical. Another way to have absolute certainty of the inner dimensions is to have an "out-of-body experience." Perhaps nothing is else is so persuasive.

When I was nineteen I was reading a book which described exercises in "astral projection"—the technique of the soul, or "astral body," lifting out of the physical body while you remain fully conscious of the experience. I tried the exercise for several weeks and one afternoon I actually began to "lift out." I was so startled by the experience that I felt momentary panic and immediately returned to my physical body. After that I stopped experimenting.

Several years later I had an out-of-body experience quite involuntarily. I was living in Europe and staying in a hotel. One night I was having difficulty sleeping due to indigestion. As I lingered in that drowsy state between wakefulness and sleep, I felt myself slip out of my physical body. Suddenly wide awake, I was thrilled to be experiencing the subtle dimension *consciously*. I realized that I was moving fluidly about in the denser levels of what is sometimes called the "etheric plane." I recognized the familiar physical environment, but in my subtle form it offered no resistance. I was quite literally going through the walls. The experience only lasted a minute or two, but it was exhilarating to say the least. Nothing is so convincing of the reality of the spiritual worlds as an experience like this one.

In the unusual book by Greta Woodrew entitled, *On a Slide of Light*, she describes her friendship with Helen Keller, who was quite elderly at the time. Helen Keller revealed to Greta Woodrew that she had become an "expert" in out-of-body projection and spent a good deal of time exploring the inner planes. Although Helen Keller lacked the sense of physical sight, she was free to perceive the multidimensional aspects of the universe through conscious activity in her subtle body. We are assured by the great spiritual guides of the human race that these experiences are the fruit of prayer, meditation, and an active inner life.

Jacques Lusseyran was a leader of the French resistance against the Nazi occupation during the second world war. He displayed daring leadership abilities and was the one his companions called upon to test if new applicants were sincere, or if they might be potential traitors to the cause. What made all this especially remarkable was that Jacques Lusseyran was blind!

Jacques had lost his eyesight in a school accident when he was eight years old. But during the years that followed he developed clairvoyant sight—the ability to "see" and perceive through inner-sensory organs of cognition. Through the intensity of his inner life, Jacques Lusseyran unfolded these higher faculties. The "gifts" of "extra-sensory perception" which he displayed are within the reach of all human beings. By going into the inner temple of our souls in periods of prayer and meditation all of us can gradually unfold the spiritual organs of perception that reveal the existence of a "higher world"—our true place of origin.

Each of us has a Sleeping Beauty in our soul. The prince whose kiss awakens Beauty is our aspiration to a higher life. As we make contact with this luminous source, the light in our minds and the love in our hearts increase. The source of life within us—the immortal spiritual spark—is an unquenchable reservoir of energy, intelligence and power. An ever-flowing spring is a beautiful symbol of this life-source. When we tap this wellspring through meditation, we release a stream of light. The light from this inner fountain becomes active in our own affairs when we express it through our words and actions.

The immortal spiritual jewel at the core of our being—our Higher Self—is like a tiny sun that radiates and gives unceasingly. This pulsating star of light within us vibrates at a very high frequency—beyond the discord of earthly conflict. To approach this center we must resonate at a high frequency in our thoughts and feelings. Those frequencies are love, wisdom, light, harmony and all the virtues of the enlightened consciousness. We know when we are beginning to resonate at these higher levels because we will experience joy and light in our consciousness. From the Higher Self radiates an endless stream of blessing. The soul is the chalice that receives the light which flows from the spiritual levels of existence. It is the symbolic Holy Grail that captures the life force and pours it out in loving service upon earth.

It is essential to form an image in meditation of one's heart center. Traditionally, the lotus, rose, or lily are recommended. When you focus the mind on such an image every day for years, you build up a powerful etheric vortex. Combined with elevated thoughts and affirmations, such exercises stimulate a miraculous transformation. You begin to weave into your subtle body the substance of your higher nature.

It has become fashionable in some circles to deny the importance of idealism, of a high ideal. Some people say that ideals and beliefs are an illusion. This viewpoint is a prescription for disaster. Without a high spiritual ideal, human beings begin to flounder, losing a sense of direction and vision. The prophet Isaiah said that "where there is no vision, the people perish." Vision comes from clear seeing. In order to see clearly we need to have a high vantage point. One can see better and farther from a high mountain than from ground level. Our ideals enable us to see far and to see clearly.

In reality, people will always have beliefs and ideals. It is the nature and quality of these beliefs and ideals which vary. Even the attitude that claims, "Beliefs are an illusion; one doesn't need them," is in itself a belief. The result of attempting to eliminate ideals will not be freedom, as some claim, but enslavement to our instinctive nature. The important thing is not to try to eliminate ideals and beliefs, but to refine and educate them. It is best if our beliefs arise from our life experiences, along with a careful contemplation of the eternal wisdom of the universal laws.

Our ideals are the subtle element that improves life and leads to better conditions. The difference between a saint and a criminal lies in their idealism. Look at what you value in your life and you will see your ideals. Even the selection of the foods we take into our body is governed by our idealism. Idealism is the star that guides our journey—the engine that directs our actions.

The high ideal is the one that believes human beings have within them a spark of greatness, a jewel of imperishable beauty. A story from India tells that when the gods created the world and the human race they wanted to give people a wealth of treasures to enjoy. But the greatest treasure of all they hid in a place where it would be difficult to find—a place where people would not think to look. So they took the greatest treasure of all, the priceless jewel of their divine nature—the very spark which was of the same immortal substance as that of which the gods were made—and this they hid within the hearts of all human beings.

The Indian spiritual teacher, H.W.L. Poonja—affectionately called Papaji—tells the following story to illustrate this truth. A master pickpocket saw a man buy the perfect diamond, one the pickpocket yearned to have. So when the man bought a train ticket to Madras, so did the pickpocket. They ended up in the same compartment. The pickpocket went through all the man's luggage and clothing when he was asleep, but he could not find the diamond. When the train reached Madras the pickpocket approached the man on the platform. "Excuse me sir," he said. "I am a master pickpocket. I have tried everything without success. You have arrived now at your destination. I will not bother you.

But I must know where you hid the diamond."

The man said, "I saw you watch me buy the diamond. When you showed up on the train, I knew you were after the diamond. I thought you must be very clever, and I wondered where I could hide this diamond that you would never search. So I hid it in your own pocket."

"The highest revelation," said Emerson, "is that God is in every man." It is this divine spark, the seed of immortality and divinity, which is gradually discovered through right living. The powers of this jewel are released as we grow inwardly through the process of prayer and meditation, and by living in a manner that serves and assists others. In our essential nature we are already perfect, whole, and complete. The deeper spiritual-self does not need improvement. It is the personality that needs to be transformed into the "temple" of the spirit. When our thoughts, feelings, and actions are harmonized with the higher frequencies of our immortal nature, the Higher Self expresses in and through us. Our Higher Self has never abandoned us. We have abandoned it. Our task is to make our personalities fit dwelling places for the eternal light. The greatest achievement, the greatest success, and the greatest miracle of any life is the discovery of one's immortal self.

The most valuable treasures in life are not material. In the words of the Little Prince, "that which is essential is invisible to the eye." The elements of highest value in life are the light of wisdom in the mind and the warmth of love in the heart. These are the heavenly treasures of ultimate worth. Just as all spectral colors are contained in the light, so are all virtues found within the light of our spirit, the light which streams through the soul in its most exalted moments.

Your progress and success in life for all time to come depends on the quality of your inner life—of your thoughts, feelings, moods and reflections. By the practice of daily reflection and study, and by periods of meditation and inner tranquillity, you begin to weave a garment of light and beauty within you. Traditionally this is called the Body of Light or the Body of Glory. In our Body of Light, or *lightbody*, we can travel at the speed of thought. Nothing of a material nature can obstruct us. Our lightbody will eventually become the vehicle in which we explore the vastness of space and the outer reaches of the universe. We build our lightbody by our best thoughts and deeds, our finest sentiments and imaginations. It is a work of many lifetimes, but the result is the creation of the garment of our immortality.

When we work consciously on creating the best within ourselves, like the butterfly, we enact the great transformation. And in so doing, we forge a bright future for ourselves and those we love.

*******

## Polishing the Jewel: Releasing the Magic of Inner Unfolding

In order to make progress in one's inner work, it is essential to set aside time for this purpose, even if for only five minutes a day. Experienced meditators, and those who establish regular time for daily periods of prayer and contemplation, often find that this quiet inner work is as necessary as eating or sleeping. The ideal is to reach the stage where making time is not an effort, but naturally becomes an essential part of the day.

There are dozens of good books on meditation, some of which you can find at any well-stocked bookstore. Generally speaking, the goal for most people, at least at first, should not be "emptying the mind." A better approach is to *focus* the mind through exercises in concentration, visualization, prayer and affirmation. Choose an uplifting thought, affirmation, or sacred image. Concentrate on it to the exclusion of all else. This is the first stage of meditation as most commonly practiced. Regarding meditative styles and techniques, much depends on one's temperament and philosophical inclinations. With practice, you will settle upon a meditative approach most suitable to your temperament and personality.

Meditation opens a window into the spiritual world. If meditation becomes a regular practice, one gradually comes to realize that the world one enters in deep contemplation is not fantasy or an illusion, but is a subtle dimension of existence that is in fact our true home and place of origin. The day is coming when people will wake up to the fact that they are not human beings having occasional spiritual experiences, but spiritual beings experiencing life on earth.

Activity # one

Find a quiet corner, relax, breathe calmly and deeply. Focus your mind upon an uplifting thought or a beautiful image—perhaps a lily, lotus or a rose. Imagine yourself sitting beside a bubbling fountain in a paradisal garden. Picture the splendor of the scenery in vivid detail. A luminous angel comes gently near and smiles. You absorb the healing, vitalizing energies that stream from the heart and head of this glorious being of love, wisdom and strength. Imagine that you are being transformed into the brilliance that lies within you as a seed—the perfection represented by the angel—an image of your own Higher Self. Slowly you are metamorphosing into this light being, becoming like the butterfly, graceful, happy and free. Resolve to express these qualities in your relationships, then open your eyes, smile and pick up the threads of living with a refreshed mind and a renewed heart.

Activity # two

This is an ancient method of mindfulness that is employed in both eastern and western traditions. Before retiring, in your mind's eye go back through the course of your day's experiences. This retrospective should be done from that moment *backwards*—almost like watching a film in reverse—until the moment you woke up. Primarily observe yourself and your reactions to people and events. What were your emotional responses? What did you say? Observe yourself from the standpoint of your Higher Self. Don't condemn yourself if you acted foolishly. Simply take note of areas where you would like to improve.

Not only will this exercise awaken your deeper self, but you will find that you fall asleep more easily and rapidly!

Affirmations

"*I am a luminous, immortal being of limitless splendor and light.*"

"*My Higher Self is perfect. I am capable of infinite expansion towards the light.*"

"*All good qualities exist now in my higher consciousness. I am in touch with this golden center of celestial perfection. I express these qualities in my life.*"

*"Every new affirmation of my celestial being is the beginning of a better life."*

# CHAPTER TWELVE
## The Twelfth Jewel — The Magic of Light

*"Can I believe what I see? All of our race proud and free!"*
— Donovan

*"Each one of you has a flame within you, and however feeble that flame may be, it is in your power to feed it until it becomes an immense blaze."* — Mikhael Aivanhov

*"Love conquers all things."* — Virgil

Light is the creative principle in nature. According to religion, the first emanation of the divine world was light. Quantum physics now recognizes that matter is really the energy of light in a more condensed or "concrete" form. What we call matter, upon close examination, displays the properties and characteristics of light. Metaphysics has always taught that light is the primordial element, and that "spirit" and "matter" are polaric expressions of this one principle. So-called matter is really "condensed" light. We live in a light-wave universe.

All the colors of the spectrum spring from the interrelation of light and darkness—of spirit and matter. Color represents the living power of the soul. The soul is the luminous child that is born of the union of spirit and matter. The more light we emanate, the more vibrant will be our soul's colors. Clairvoyants see these colors in our aura. Some intuitives can diagnose our health from the colors of our energy field. As we work to improve our inner life we enhance the beauty of our soul's emanations. We create a spectrum of living light in our consciousness. This is the way of transformation—the path of light.

Physics recognizes that there are light-wave frequencies above that of visible light on the electromagnetic spectrum. This fact in nature is symbolic of the subtle qualities of light which emanate from the soul and spirit dimensions. The invisible light-wave frequencies correspond to the most luminous, yet subtle, radiations of thought and emotion.

*Light* has a dual meaning. Used as a noun, *light* is radiance, or illumination. Used as an adjective it refers to the absence of weight. Thus it is associated both with intelligence (the light of knowledge) and with freedom (the lack of burdens). What we call enlightenment is a process of introducing more light into our thinking and our emotions, which will result in light-filled actions. It is a process of illumination and liberation. Our thoughts and feelings determine the quality and quantity of the light we emanate and express in our lives.

In ancient times men and women searched on the external plane for the Fountain of Youth. The Fountain of Youth will not be found in the physical world. It is in yourself that its eternal waters flow. The Fountain of Youth is the light that springs forever from the core of our spirit self. When we produce luminous thoughts and warm positive feelings, we bathe in the immortal fountain that springs from within our hearts.

Angels and spiritual beings have always been described in

terms of their light—what is often characterized as an almost blinding radiance. So luminous was Christ at the moment of his transfiguration that the disciples had to shield their eyes. *Deva*, the Sanskrit term for angel, means "shining one."

The light of intellectual knowledge alone is a cold light; it does not stir the heart. For light to touch the heart it must be filled with warmth—the warmth of love. Light is closely related to love. They are expressions of the same force. The radiance of light and the warmth of love spring from the fire of our spirit—the divine spark within each of us—our true self. When expressed through the mind, spiritual energy becomes intelligence, or wisdom. This inner beauty expressed through the heart becomes the warmth of love and joy. Our spiritual essence is both radiance and warmth—wisdom and love.

Several years ago, Suzanne Ciani composed a beautiful melody entitled *The Velocity of Love*. We often hear references to the speed of light, but we rarely think in terms of love having velocity. Her song made me think. Does love have a velocity? If so, is it greater than the speed of light?

We know that love can heal, and that young children deprived of love begin to wither and die. What other unknown powers and qualities might love contain? In her inspired book, *Mary's Message to the World*, Annie Kirkwood describes the undiscovered powers of love that will become known in the near future. She confirms that love has a velocity greater than that of light. She even makes the startling statement that it will be possible to heat our homes wtih the energy of love! Love has a measurable vibrational field. Love can penetrate the most formidable barriers. There is no place in the universe that love cannot go. Love is the quintessence of life itself.

In his brilliant book, *The Fruit of Your Thoughts*, John Roberts paraphrases Peter Rosen's words on loving and enlightened living:

"We evolve spiritually by developing the courage to love, which rids us of fear. Recognize and accept that God is the one energy that fills us all. Just be yourself. We don't have to prove that we are loving. Love is our energy. We show this through our respect and courage.

"With nothing to defend and to lose, we can be like the Master and exude peace. Silence speaks loudly...There is no danger when you are safely cradled in the arms of love...Remind yourself to be relaxed, loving and kind today."

If we embrace the love and light of our deeper self, we can alter our destiny. By loving actions we can dissolve potential dangers on our path. This is one of the meanings of divine grace. We activate the power of divine grace when we consistently express the magic of love. When we fill our minds with the wisdom of luminous thinking, the petals of our hearts begin to blossom. Just as plants turn toward the light of the sun, so do our hearts open to the sun of love that shines eternally from our divine self.

The greatest mystery and the greatest power in life is that of love. It is the greatest power because it is stronger than any other emotion, and can transform the most wretched individual and redeem the most difficult circumstances. It is the greatest mystery, for we know so little about the higher nature of love and have only begun in the most fumbling fashion to express it.

The Greeks had several words to express different manifestations of love. Sexual love was *Eros*. *Philia* meant a love as might be shared between long-time friends, or by members of the same family who felt strong feelings of kinship. *Agape* referred to the highest form of love—an ideal, transcendent, spiritual love.

Christ said to love God with all your mind, heart, soul, and strength, and to love your neighbor as yourself. A saintly love as expressed by Jesus, Buddha and Saint Francis is indeed rare, if not altogether nonexistent. Yet many individuals have reached a point in their development where love for others—and the ideal of expressing love—is becoming the prime motivating force in their lives. Love gives hope to all. It is the promise that keeps one striving, growing, and becoming.

When I was a teenager, I sometimes reflected on the words that my "angel presence" spoke to me when I was five years old. "You are on earth to learn to love." I thought then that it was an easy thing to love. Only with the tests and challenges of adult life did I realize that to love was not as simple as my youthful idealism had believed. The mind is always coming up with a multitude of reasons why we shouldn't love. And the fact is that human beings are all so very different. If we focus on the differences and the abrasive little peculiarities of human personality, we're likely to throw up our arms in exasperation. If we care to look, we can always find a significant number of "revolting specimens" in the world. The harsh experiences and disappointments of life can easily make us bitter. But only by loving can we free ourselves from negative emotions and the shackles of our critical minds.

I know two women who are an inspiring example of the power of love. Marge and Mary are "getting old" but are very youthful in spirit. A few years ago they decided to go to Britain together. They rented a car and spent two weeks touring Ireland, Scotland, Wales, and England. They are both strong and independent personalities, and held differing opinions of how to "have a good time" on their vacation abroad. When they returned it was easy to see that they had sometimes rubbed on each other's nerves.

A year later Marge had a stroke and a heart attack, followed by quadruple bypass surgery. There was a great outpouring of affection for her from her community of friends. One of the most steadfast, loyal, and attentive was Mary. She was at Marge's side day and night. It was heartwarming to see the bond of love they shared. Marge was soon back on her feet after a recovery which was a miracle in its own right. I saw them together one evening and Mary jokingly "complained" of all she did to help Marge when she was bed-ridden. She smiled at Marge, then added with a gleam in her eyes, "But would I do it again?" She paused a moment, then warmly exclaimed, "Yes, you bet I would!"

Love is a power that can transform the sorrowful experiences of life. But the difficulties we experience are not in themselves a badge of honor. I have known people whose lives have been very difficult and who seem to think they have somehow earned great merit as a result of their suffering. But the difficulties we endure are not the factor in life of greatest significance. More important is the manner in which we respond to life's challenges. As a friend of mine, Alan Greene, has so wisely said, "It is not how much we have suffered in life that matters most, but how much we have loved."

Much of the suffering people experience is due to a misunderstanding of love. "The misfortunes of people today," said the inspired teacher, Peter Deunov, "are due to the fact that they do not manifest their love, but rather expect others to love them. The disenchantment of people is due to the fact that they expect to be loved. Those who want the love of others, but do not give of themselves, cannot be loved. Let them first give their love and it will be given unto them. Unless you first give your heart, you will always be far from love...as soon as you find love, you will know the inner meaning of life. In this way you will love everything in the world; animals, plants and even every stone. Love everything but do not strive to possess anything."

Love is always expressed through giving. Giving is the spontaneous outgrowth of love. For love to transform the world, it must shine through our generosity. The ancient Egyptian image mentioned in Chapter Four, of the sun with many rays—and a hand on the end of each ray—is a beautiful picture of the givingness of light and love. The sun is the heart of our solar system. It overflows with generosity, and gives life to all by its constant outpouring of warmth and light.

Those who focus on light-filled thoughts kindle a flame within their consciousness which can grow in intensity and illuminate the whole of life. Such people become beacons of light in the subtle dimensions. As you send forth loving emanations, you are bathed in ethereal light. When one releases the light, one receives it.

When you love something, you begin to resemble it. If we love art, music, athletics, literature or anything—we may begin to acquire skills and talents in that area. Love awakens slumbering faculties, even genius. If you want to obtain anything of value in life, you must love it, because love is the most magnetic force in existence. Mastery in any area of life is the fruit of love.

The mysterious motive power at the core of human feeling is love. Love gives vitality to life. It is the driving force in human evolution. Within nature, love is the divine play of all elements and all creatures—the heavenly *Lila*, or dance, of Indian mythology.

In human relationships love is the rhythmic dance of giving and receiving—of balanced, kind-hearted exchanges. Expressing goodwill and helpfulness liberates one from the prison of loneliness and despair. Love is also the most important element in any spiritual practice. In the words of Sai Baba, "Begin the day with love, fill the day with love, end the day with love. This is the way to God-consciousness." The more love we infuse into our labors, the more happiness we experience. The feeling of love in the heart is the source of contentment in life. Love is the wellspring of human joy.

One of the most beautiful and loving relationships that has come down to us from the past is that of Robert Browning and Elizabeth Barret Browning, two of England's most significant nineteenth century poets. Elizabeth was petite, and because of her olive complexion, Robert affectionately called her "my little Portuguese." Her famous verses published under the title, *Sonnets From the Portuguese*, have always been among the world's most beloved poems.

When Elizabeth's health deteriorated, Robert arranged for them to travel to Italy in the hope that the warmer climate would restore her. Her health returned and they decided to live in Italy. They built a home in Florence where they spent the happiest years of their life together. But in June of 1861, Elizabeth again became ill. This time Robert knew intuitively that she would not recover. All night he sat beside her bed, praying passionately, imploring her not to leave him. Occasionally she would recover from her sleep and gently smile or whisper a word of hope until she was too weak even for that. Late at night she recovered enough to ask him to hold her one last time. She could barely whisper the words, "Hold me, beloved." He lifted her from the bed and carried her to the chair by the window, cradling her gently in his arms until dawn. As the first light of the new day touched the sky, he kissed her on her cold lips one last time. She stirred from her deep sleep and whispered her final words, "It is beautiful," then passed away.

Through his grief Robert Browning wrote one of his greatest poems, *Prospice* (look forward) in which he scribed his conviction that love is eternal and that he would one day again hold his beloved in his arms. He wrote, "Oh thou soul of my soul! I shall clasp thee again." No doubt he was inspired by the lines of one of Elizabeth's most universally loved poems, written for him and published in *Sonnets From the Portuguese*.

> "I love thee with the breath,
> Smiles, tears, of all my life! — and if God choose,
> I shall love thee better after death."

Robert and Elizabeth Barret Browning knew what all mystics, saints, and visionary poets have known—that love is an eternal force that overcomes death. Truly, those who love never die.

Love transforms the experience of human life. Love is an elevated state of consciousness that is always expressed in harmonious actions and gestures. The feeling of expansion and well-being that comes when we experience love in our hearts is its own reward. Mikhael Aivhanov, the inspired Bulgarian teacher and philosopher, expressed these words about the power of love: "Our hearts must be full of love for human beings because they are all our brothers and sisters. We must think of them and help them without expecting the slightest reward, for, in reality, our reward is already given to us in that inner sense of expansion, that extraordinary sensation of warmth that fills us when we love. This is a marvelous reward; life contains none greater."

A day will come when science understands love to be a cosmic force that flows through all dimensions of life. Love is the supreme light and energy which makes existence possible and without which there could be no life.

The drop of elixir extracted from the grinding wheels of destiny is wisdom-filled love—the quintessence of experience. Light and love give wings to the mind and the imagination, enabling the soul to rise to a higher state of awareness and behold the image of its own divinity.

Life without love is a wasteland. Where love is expressed a fountain bursts forth and an oasis comes to life. When the earth is filled with countless of these fountains of light—these springs of kindness—then the earth will become once again a garden.

In an age to come, humanity will resolve all conflicting tones and discord into a vibrant harmony. It was this vision that inspired Beethoven to write the choral finale to his Ninth Symphony, the famous *Ode to Joy*. Already a fortunate few on earth can hear the faint strains of the new music sounding in the depths of their consciousness. These are the advance guard of the coming race of enlightened humanity. In the future we will move to the rhythms and will give voice to the inspirations of light-filled love. It is this world that seeks to come to birth through humankind.

Christ gave the secret to enlightenment and liberation when he said, "Love one another as I have loved you." St. John the Divine echoed these words when he wrote, "Let us love one another, for love is of God...If we love one another, God lives in us, and divine love is perfected in us." These words are the capstone on the monument to wisdom entrusted to us by the ancient world. They are also a revelation illuminating our path into the future. Love is the key that unlocks the portals to heaven on earth. When we vibrate to the melody of love, we resonate in harmony with the entire universe.

When we finally walk in harmony with the rhythms of this celestial power, we will give expression to the vision of the immortal Italian poet, Dante Alighieri, when he wrote the final words of his *Divine Comedy*, "My will and my desire were turned by love, the love that moves the sun and the other stars."

*******

**Polishing the Jewel: Releasing the Magic of Light**

Activity # one

Sit comfortably in your favorite chair. Imagine that your real being is weightless and luminous. Even your physical body is fundamentally composed of light. Affirm that the universe we live in is a light-wave universe. Your thoughts are subtle frequencies of light.

Visualize a star of light or a radiant sun above your head. This represents your Higher Self—who you are in essence. (It is helpful to picture this star above you often during the day and during times of meditation and inner quiet.) Imagine that streams of wisdom, love and strength flow from this star into your mind, heart and physical body. All the cells of your body are bathed in this beautiful, healing light. Darkness vanishes. You are in perfect health—an eternal being of light, now and forevermore.

Activity # two

Stand in front of an open window and breathe deeply. Picture the golden star of your Higher Self just above you. Imagine that on each inbreath you are pulling in a stream of golden light from this star. The stream of light flows down into the region of your heart. As you gently breathe out, imagine that this light is streaming forth in all directions as love from your heart. Imagine that it is stimulating the light in the minds and the warmth in the hearts of all creatures everywhere. You can do this exercise as often as you like. You should find that it has a tremendous power to stimulate your own inner unfolding.

## Activity # three

Relax in your customary place of quiet and meditation. Breathe slowly and deeply, mentally repeating affirmations or prayers that help you achieve a calm and uplifted state of mind. Then picture yourself in a vast meadow of grass and flowers. These can be tulips, lilies, irises, roses, or any flower you desire. See yourself walking through the meadow towards a hill in the direction of the sunrise. Just as you reach the top of the hill the sun appears in all its brilliance above the horizon. In the valley beneath you, spread before your delighted and astounded eyes, is a serene community of the future. In the center of the valley is a glorious temple that appears to built of purest, gleaming gold. You have entered the earth of a future epoch—a golden age of universal peace, goodwill, and prosperity. All nations have learned to live in amity, and blood is no longer shed upon the earth.

Picture in great detail the wonderful and inspiring advances of this enlightened civilization. What will the architecture be like? What are people wearing? Picture the health and happiness of all the people you see. Know that you are a beloved member of this coming, illuminated humanity.

Exercises like this one help to build the thoughtform of the new civilization and strengthen your own subconscious assurance of better times to come.

## Affirmations

*"I am a ray of luminous love—happy, brilliant and weightless."*

*"I live in the light. I am a child of limitless light and universal love."*

*"I transform my environment into a kingdom of light and happiness. May all those with whom I am and ever will be in contact be blessed."*

*"May my heart shine with love for all beings."*

## AFTERWARD
## The Synthesis of the Jewels

When you put together a puzzle, there is a defining moment when suddenly the entire picture can be visualized. Each of the preceding chapters is a piece of a puzzle whose entirety forms a complete image—an image of a harmonious life characterized by light, kindness, and gentle strength.

When you have completed this book, you may wish to read it again immediately in order to absorb these "jewels" more deeply into your mind. To derive maximum benefit from each chapter, it is suggested that you spend a week focusing on each jewel. An excellent practice is to read a chapter in the morning as soon as you awake, and again in the evening before retiring. As you do so, your understanding will increase. The light in your mind will grow as you imprint these laws into your heart through concentration and reflection.

Try to put into practice the ideas of each chapter. Keep a notebook or diary of your insights and recollections. Reflect on your daily experiences and interactions in the light of each jewel. In some areas you will be stronger than others. For instance, you may tend to be an "idea person," always thinking and conceptualizing, but not very effective in getting things done and carrying through with decisions. If that is the case, spend more time on chapter four, the magic of action. Work more intensively with the affirmations at the end of that chapter, and make up affirmations of your own that will develop in your personality the qualities you desire.

It is especially effective if you work with these ideas in a small study group formed for this purpose. Each member will have unique insights and experiences that will add to the understanding of everyone. It is possible to think these truths deeply into the subconscious mind where they become a permanent feature of character. Each individual who does so will be performing a work upon themselves that will benefit everyone. The more people who grasp and apply the deeper truths—the laws that form the foundation of life—the sooner humankind can solve its problems and enter a more harmonious era.

The world today is in the midst of unprecedented turmoil and upheaval. At the same time, there is recognition of a global spiritual awakening—often referred to as a shift in human perception. These seemingly contrary developments should come as no surprise, for we stand at a historical turning point. It is as if we have entered the turbulent waters where two oceans meet. The human race is moving out of one experience into an entirely new world, with fresh currents leading us to undiscovered possibilities. If we can solve our present challenges, we will find ourselves on the threshold of a new era in human understanding and achievement. In order to move through the current crisis, there must be a core group of individuals—a vanguard—who can lead the way into more peaceful waters.

The coming transformation in consciousness is often described as a collective experience that will be made by the entire human race. But the human race is made up of individuals. Just as each child must learn to walk on his own, so must we—*as individuals*—take the first steps into a more enlightened life.

What is required is a sufficient number of daring individuals with awakened hearts and pioneer spirits—men and women who can anchor the new consciousness in their daily lives.

Ultimately, each person is meant to transform his or her own soul into a "jewel." This jewel may be visualized as having twelve facets. Each facet represents one of the twelve magical laws described in this book. Thus, it is a synthesis of all the jewels—a single gem of indescribable brilliance.

An image of this 12-fold perfection is the *dodecahedron*, pictured below and at the beginning of each chapter of this book. The dodecahedron is one of the five geometric shapes known collectively as the "Platonic solids." Plato, the illustrious Athenian philosopher for whom these shapes were named, said that God used the dodecahedron when he created the world and set the constellations in the heavens. This image is a fitting symbol for the jewel of our inner self—our true divine nature—which shines with an eternal star-like brilliance.

There is a transcendent wisdom that underlies our universe. It bursts forth from an eternal spring that streams out of the heart of the world. The living water from this fountain is the source of life and light that sustains all creatures. Humanity's age-long thirst will be quenched when it finds this water of life. In so doing we will come to understand the great laws that govern existence. The living synthesis of all these laws is love. May all people discover and apply these truths, so that we may begin to transform this earth into the garden it is meant to become.

### Meditative Verse

More radiant than the sun,
Purer than the snow,
Finer than the ether,
is the Self,
The Spirit in my heart.
This Self am I
I am this self.

—Rudolf Steiner

# Suggested Reading

Aivanhov, Omraam M. *The Book of Divine Magic*. France: Editions Prosveta, 1989.

Aivanhov, Omraam M. *Golden Rules for Everyday Life*. France: Editions Prosveta , 1990.

Anderson, Greg. *The 22 (Non-Negotiable) Laws of Wellness*. New York: Harper Collins, 1995.

Brinkley, Dannion. *Saved By the Light*. New York: Villard Books, 1995.

Burnham, Sophie. *Book of Angels*. New York: Ballantine, 1990, 1994.

Canfield, Jack and Hansen, Mark Victor. *Chicken Soup For the Soul*. Deerfield Beach, Florida: Health Communications, 1993.

Carter, Forrest. *The Education of LittleTree*. Albuquerque, NM: University of New Mexico Press, 1976.

Charlton, Hilda. *Saints Alive*. Woodstock, NY: Golden Quest, 1989.

Clark, Glenn. *The Man Who Tapped the Secrets of the Universe*. Swannanoa, Virginia: University of Science and Philosophy, 1946.

Cohen, Alan. *The Dragon Doesn't Live Here Anymore*. New York: Fawcett Columbine, 1981.

Dossey, Larry. *Healing Words*. New York: Harper Collins, 1993.

Easwaran, Eknath. Editor, *The Dhammapada*. Tomales, CA: Nilgiri Press, 1985.

Hamilton, Edith. *Mythology*. New York: Penguin Meridain, 1969.

Hay, Louise. *You Can Heal Your Life*. Carlsbad, CA: Hay House, 1984,1987.

Hill, Napoleon. *Think and Grow Rich*. New York: Fawcett Crest, 1963.

Holmes, Ernest. *Science of Mind*. New York: G.P. Putnam and Sons, 1938, 1966.

190

Isherwood, Christopher and Prabhavananda, Swami. *The Song of God: The Bhagavad Gita*. New York: Penguin Books, 1944, 1972.

King, Serge. *Mastering Your Hidden Self*. Wheaton, Illinois: Quest Books, 1985.

Lorimer, David. *Prophet For Our Times: The Life and Teachings of Peter Deunov*. Rockport, MA. Element, 1991.

Lusseyran, Jacques. *And There Was Light*. California: Atrium, 1986.

Markides, Kyriacos. *The Magus of Strovolos*. New York: Arcana/Penguin, 1985.

Mitchell. Stephen, editor. *Tao Te Ching*. New York: Harper Collins, 1988.

Myss, Caroline. *Anatomy of the Spirit*. New York: Harmony Books, 1996.

Robbins, Anthony. *Unlimited Power*. New York: Ballantine, 1986.

Roberts, John. *The Fruit of Your Thoughts*. Boise, Idaho: Roaring Lion Publishing. 1997.

Rosen, Peter. *Luminous Life*. Gatlinburg, TN: Roaring Lion Publishers, 1995.

Russell, Lao. *God Will Work With You But Not For You*. Waynesboro, Virginia: University of Science and Philosophy, 1955.

Sardello, Robert. *Love and the Soul*. New York: Harper Collins, 1995.

Steiner, Rudolf. *Knowledge of Higher Worlds and its Attainment*. New York: Anthroposophic Press, 1947.

White Eagle. *Wisdom From White Eagle*. Hampshire, England: White Eagle Publishing Trust, 1967.

White Eagle. *The Quiet Mind*. Hampshire, England: White Eagle Publishing Trust, 1972.

Zitko, John. *Lemurian Theo-Christic Conception*. Benson, Arizona: World University, 1964.

To order any of the above titles, consult your local bookstore, or call 520-445-5056.

# ORDER FORM

Mountain Rose Publishing Company
PO Box 2738
Prescott, AZ 86302
(520)445-5056
FAX (520)778-1601

To order more copies of JEWELS OF LIGHT, or Emory John Michael's exciting spiritual adventure, QUEEN OF THE SUN, fill in the information below and send it in with a check, or just pick up the phone and order with a credit card. Call 520-445-5056.

| QUANTITY | TITLE | AMOUNT |
|---|---|---|
| _____ | JEWELS OF LIGHT @ 12.00 | _____ |
| _____ | QUEEN OF THE SUN @ $12.95 | _____ |

Shipping:          $2.00 first book                                   _____
                         $1.00 second book                           _____
                         $0.50 each additional book               _____
Arizona residents add 7.0% sales tax                          _____
Amount enclosed (U.S. Funds)                                    _____

Name: _____

Address: _____

_____

Phone (____) _____

I can't wait 2-4 weeks for book rate. Here is $3.00 per book for air mail/first class To speed up phone orders please have credit card number ready:

Only the dreamer can change the dream.
Only the thinker can change the thought.
Only you can change your personal world.

# ABOUT THE AUTHOR

Emory John Michael has spent many years living and travel-ing abroad—much of that time in Europe and South America. He has a degree in education and has taught students of all ages in a variety of settings and countries. While living in Europe, he taught English as a second language in Rome, Spain, and Switzerland. His first book, QUEEN OF THE SUN, is currently being translated into nine foreign languages. He has appeared on radio and TV shows across the country, and teaches classes and seminars on the material in his books.

Mr. Michael and his talented wife, Mia, own a book and gift store in Prescott, Arizona. When not writing, playing music, or traveling, he enjoys exploring the National Forest by their home—a high desert treasure-trove of natural splendors. Mr. Michael publishes a quarterly newsletter, called *The Oracle*.

To be on Emory John Michael's mailing list and receive his quarterly newsletter, please send $16.00 to Mountain Rose Publishing, PO Box 2738, Prescott, AZ 86302